PENGUIN BOOKS

COMPLETE LYRICS 1978–2013

CW01597298

Nick Cave w … ndon with his band The Bi … rmed The Bad Seeds, with … ns. In 1999 he curated the … Bank Centre. His novels … *of Bunny Munro* (2009) were international bestsellers. … *osition* appeared to wide critical acclaim in 2005, while his band Grinderman have released two albums. Nick Cave lives on the South Coast of England.

The Complete Lyrics 1978–2013

Nick Cave

PENGUIN BOOKS

PENGUIN BOOKS

Published by the Penguin Group
Penguin Books Ltd, 80 Strand, London WC2R 0RL, England
Penguin Group (USA) Inc., 375 Hudson Street, New York, New York 10014, USA
Penguin Group (Canada), 90 Eglinton Avenue East, Suite 700, Toronto, Ontario, Canada M4P 2Y3
(a division of Pearson Penguin Canada Inc.)
Penguin Ireland, 25 St Stephen's Green, Dublin 2, Ireland (a division of Penguin Books Ltd)
Penguin Group (Australia), 707 Collins Street, Melbourne, Victoria 3008, Australia
(a division of Pearson Australia Group Pty Ltd)
Penguin Books India Pvt Ltd, 11 Community Centre,
Panchsheel Park, New Delhi – 110 017, India
Penguin Group (NZ), 67 Apollo Drive, Rosedale, Auckland 0632, New Zealand
(a division of Pearson New Zealand Ltd)
Penguin Books (South Africa) (Pty) Ltd, Block D, Rosebank Office Park,
181 Jan Smuts Avenue, Parktown North, Gauteng 2193, South Africa

Penguin Books Ltd, Registered Offices: 80 Strand, London WC2R 0RL, England

www.penguin.com

First published in Penguin Books 2001
Second edition 2007
This revised and updated edition published 2013

003

Copyright © Mute Song Ltd, 2001, 2007, 2013
Foreword copyright © Will Self, 2007
All rights reserved

The moral right of the author has been asserted

All individual lyrics copyright © Mute Song Ltd, reproduced by permission, except 'Mr Clarinet' and 'Happy Birthday', reproduced by kind permission of Complete Music Ltd, and 'The Friend Catcher' by kind permission of Beggars Banquet Music.

'A Dead Song', 'Dead Joe', 'Truck Love', 'Kiss Me Black', 'From Her to Eternity' and 'Tread Softly (In Love)' by Nick Cave with Anita Lane. 'Gun Play #3' by Nick Cave with Lydia Lunch. 'Wings Off Flies' by Nick Cave with Peter Sutcliffe. 'Henry Lee' traditional, with Nick Cave.
'Better the Devil You Know', written by Stock, Aitken and Waterman, appears with permission of Mike Stock Publishing Limited, Sids Songs Limited, BMG Music Publishing Limited and All Boys Music Limited.

Printed and bound in Great Britain by Clays Ltd, Elcograf S.p.A.

Except in the United States of America, this book is sold subject to the condition that it shall not, by way of trade or otherwise, be lent, re-sold, hired out, or otherwise circulated without the publisher's prior consent in any form of binding or cover other than that in which it is published and without a similar condition including this condition being imposed on the subsequent purchaser

ISBN: 978–0–241–97964–8

www.greenpenguin.co.uk

FSC www.fsc.org
MIX
Paper from responsible sources
FSC™ C018179

Penguin Books is committed to a sustainable future for our business, our readers and our planet. This book is made from Forest Stewardship Council™ certified paper.

'And I only am escaped to tell thee' – JOB

Contents

Foreword
Will Self

Some twenty years ago I had a long wrangle with the music writer Barney Hoskyns about the relative virtues of rock lyricists. Barney's view was (and I hope I'm not traducing him in any way) that simplicity is the key. The structure of pop songs – most of which derive from the holy miscegenation of the English ballad form and the eight-bar blues – the importance to them of melody, and their fairly short duration: all of these factors meant that facile rhymes, basic narratives and straightforward sentiments made for the best lyrics.

In view of this, Barney championed the writing of Smokey Robinson. Indeed, he went further, saying that Robinson was incomparably the best post-war pop lyricist. Perhaps to be contrary – or maybe because I genuinely believed it, it's so difficult to tell sometimes – I passionately dissented from this view, arguing that a lyricist such as Bob Dylan managed to be at once experimental and deeply poetic, while still packing a perfectly sweet pop punch to the gut.

As I recall, the argument eventually came down to a single couplet from Dylan's song 'Visions of Johanna': 'On the back of the fish truck that loads / While my conscience explodes.' Barney contended that this, in and of itself, meant absolutely nothing at all. Therefore, it could only be viewed either as a self-indulgent verbal riff, or as filler, marking time until the beat cranked up again.

Being forced to analyse the meaning of this trope was, initially, unwelcome. I had no desire to descend either into the nerdish, psycho-biographical slough of the Dylanologists, nor ascend to the arid heights of those academics, who have hung on to their tenure by maintaining the view that some songwriters may be considered quite as much 'poets' as their unaccompanied counterparts. As far as I'm concerned, this approach has always begged the question: if lyricists are poets, then what are poets – presumably one-man bands without a band?

Over the past two decades, to my own satisfaction, at least, I've come up with not just one viable interpretation of the vexed unloading fish truck, but many. Moreover, I've come to an understanding of the nature and purpose of lyrics that satisfies me, while incidentally explaining the collapse of poetry as a popular art form. Nowadays, if we picture the poetic muse at all, it's as a superannuated folkie, sitting in the corner of the literary lounge bar, holding his ear and yodelling some old bollocks or other. Whatever need we have for the esemplastic unities of sound, meaning and rhythm that were traditionally supplied by spoken verse, we now find, amply, in sung lyrics.

Curiously, it was also Hoskyns, a couple of years before, who nearly effected an introduction between me and a young Australian punk band that he was then in the process of championing. I was hanging out with a mutual friend, lost in the toxic imbroglio of those telescopic times, when the invitation came to head up to Clapham and meet the Birthday Party. We never made it. We never got our £10 party bag.

I was aware of Nick Cave, of course, his incendiary performances – setting fire to the Gothic catafalque above Pop's tomb, and writhing as it burned, burned, burned – were a defining part of the same, troubled era. However, I came to the music itself late. Indeed, I knew Nick himself, socially, long before I immersed myself in his oeuvre. Looking back on that time – the late 1980s and early 1990s – this seems staggering. I'm often reminded of the first line of Woody Allen's parody of Albert Speer's disingenuous memoir: 'I did not know Hitler was a Nazi. The truth was, for years I thought he worked for the phone company.'

I may not have thought Nick Cave worked for the phone company, but I had no conception of the extent to which his creative gestalt was shot through by harmony quite as much as semantics. He was an affable – if gaunt – bloke I saw at barbecues with his kids.

Then I read his novel *And the Ass Saw the Angel*, and was exposed, full force, to the great, Manichean divide that rives the Cave worldview. Exposed also to his very individual and mythopoeic terrain: a landscape, present in his songs and his prose alike, wherein sex kicks up the dust, murders take place in the heat (of the moment), and the sins of the fathers are visited on everyone. To those unfamiliar with the very particularity of the Australian hinterland – both physical and cultural – the backdrop to many Cave ballads, with their talk of guns, knives, horses and brides, may seem cut from a similar cloth to that of lyricists such as Johnny Cash, Bob Dylan, and the blues men and country artists they revere.

Not so. Cave's *mise en scène* is as particular to his Australian patrimony as the whorls are to his fingers, or his lexicon is to his idiolect. Here, in rural Victoria, the light is harsher, the flies' legs are moister and the blood takes longer to coagulate. A persistent atmosphere of the uncanny pervades the world the songster summons up, and while immersed in a Cave lyric, it's easy to believe, not only in full temporal simultaneity – the indigenes are hacked to death, even as a football is kicked across the oval – but also that this sepia land marches with ancient Israel itself, both the Pharisees and the Kelly Gang, having been clamped by the neck for the time necessary to secure a group portrait.

So, it would be invidious for me to quote from the lyrics in this volume; and given what I've stated above, otiose to offer close analysis of them. Suffice to say, Cave, as a poetic craftsman, provides all the enjambment, ellipsis and onomatopoeia that anyone could wish for. However, I suspect that most who buy this book will not be intending to read it in such a way; rather, it is an album of lyrical portraiture, all of them bearing a family resemblance, yet all of distinct phenotypes. The joy lies in relating each to the other, building the connections. And, of course, in hearing the melodies in one's inner ear.

A word on eroticism and the dreadful dolour of knowing not only that all passion is spent – but also that you're overdrawn. If Cave were to be typified as a lyricist of blood, guts and angst it would be a grave mistake. He stands as one of the great writers on love of our era. Each Cave love song is at once perfumed with yearning, and already stinks of the putrefying loss-to-come. For Cave, consummation is always exactly that.

I don't want to go without also signing a vein of irony – satire even – that runs through Nick Cave's lyrics. One of my personal favourites, 'God is in the House', demonstrates his ability to ironize, then re-ironize, and then re-ironize again, engendering a dizzying vortex as received values are sucked down the pointed plughole. Arguably, such a light-heavyweight touch runs counter to Cave's espousal of the Old Testament verities, yet I prefer to acknowledge it as of a piece: *Ecce homo*.

So, in the last analysis, it seems that the decades-old wrangle about lyricists was quite as devoid of meaning as the unloading fish truck, for, at that very time, in the existential inner cities of London, Berlin, New York, Paris, there was tapping away a songwriter who was far more than the sum of these parts: the aching heart of Smokey, implanted in the tortured breast of Zimmerman.

WWS, London 2007

The Secret Life of the Love Song

West Country Girl

With a crooked smile and a heart-shaped face
Comes from the West Country where the birds sing bass
She's got a house-big heart where we all live
And plead and counsel and forgive
Her widow's peak, her lips I've kissed
Her glove of bones at her wrist
That I have held in my hand
Her Spanish fly and her monkey gland
Her Godly body and its fourteen stations
That I have embraced, her palpitations
Her unborn baby crying, 'Mummy'
Amongst the rubble of her body
Her lovely lidded eyes I've sipped
Her fingernails, all pink and chipped
Her accent which I'm told is 'broad'
That I have heard and has been poured
Into my human heart and filled me
With love, up to the brim, and killed me
And rebuilt me back anew
With something to look forward to
Well, who could ask much more than that?
A West Country girl with a big fat cat
That looks into her eyes of green
And meows, 'He loves you,' then meows again

That was a song called 'West Country Girl'. It is a Love Song.

It began, in its innocence, as a poem, written about two years ago in Australia, where the sun shines. I wrote it with my heart in my mouth, detailing in list form the physical details which drew me toward a particular person . . . the West Country Girl. It set forth my own personal criteria of beauty, my own particular truth about beauty, as angular, cruel and impoverished as it probably was. It was a list of things I loved, and, in truth, a wretched exercise in flattery, designed to win the girl. And it worked and it didn't work. But the peculiar magic of the Love Song, if it has the heart to do it, is that it *endures* where the object of the song does not. It attaches itself to you and together you move through time. But it does more than that, for just as it is our task to move forward, to cast off our past, to change and to grow, in short, to forgive ourselves and each other, the Love Song holds within it an eerie intelligence all of its own – to reinvent the past and to lay it at the feet of the present.

'West Country Girl' began in innocence and in sunshine, as a simple poem about a girl. But it has done what all true Love Songs must do in order to survive, it has demanded the right to its own identity, its own life, its own truth. I've seen it grow and mutate with time. It presents itself now as a cautionary tale, as a list of ingredients in a witches' brew, it reads as a coroner's report, or a message on a sandwich-board worn by a wild-eyed man who states, 'The End of the World is at Hand.' It is a hoarse voice in the dark that croaks, 'Beware . . . beware . . . beware.'

Anyway, I'm getting ahead of myself. My name is Nick Cave, and I've got a few things to tell you.

People Ain't No Good

People just ain't no good
I think that's well understood
You can see it everywhere you look
People just ain't no good

We were married under cherry trees
Under blossom we made our vows
All the blossoms come sailing down
Through the streets and through the playgrounds

The sun would stream on the sheets
Awoken by the morning bird
We'd buy the Sunday newspapers
And never read a single word

People they ain't no good
People they ain't no good
People they ain't no good

Seasons came, seasons went
The winter stripped the blossoms bare
A different tree now lines the streets
Shaking its fists in the air

The winter slammed us like a fist
The windows rattling in the gales
To which she drew the curtains
Made out of her wedding veils

People they ain't no good
People they ain't no good
People they ain't no good

To our love send a dozen white lilies
To our love send a coffin of wood
To our love let all the pink-eyed pigeons coo
That people they just ain't no good
To our love send back all the letters
To our love a valentine of blood
To our love let all the jilted lovers cry
That people they just ain't no good

It ain't that in their hearts they're bad
They can comfort you, some even try
They nurse you when you're ill of health
They bury you when you go and die
It ain't that in their hearts they're bad
They'd stick by you if they could
But that's just bullshit, baby
People just ain't no good

People they ain't no good
People they ain't no good
People they ain't no good
People they ain't no good

I performed an earlier, more conservative, lo-tech version of this lecture at the Poetry Academy in Vienna last year. I was invited to go there and actually *teach* a group of adult students about song-writing. But first they wanted me to give a public lecture. The subject I chose was the Love Song, and in doing it – I mean, standing up in front of a crowd of people and *teaching, lecturing* – I was filled with a host of conflicting feelings. The strongest, most insistent of these feelings was one of abject *horror*. Horror, because my late father was an English-literature teacher at the highschool I attended back in Australia – you know, where the sun shines. I have very clear memories of being about twelve years old and sitting, as you are now, in a classroom or hall, watching my father, who would be standing, up here, where I am standing, and thinking to myself, gloomily and miserably – for, in the main, I was a gloomy and miserable child – 'It doesn't really matter what I do with my life as long as I don't end up like my father.' Now, at forty-one years old, it would appear that there is virtually no action I can take that does not draw me closer to him, that does not make me more like him. At forty-one years of age I have become my father, and here I am, ladies and gentlemen, *teaching*.

Looking back over the last twenty years a certain clarity prevails. Amidst the madness and the mayhem, it would seem I have been banging on one particular drum. I see that my artistic life has centred around an attempt to articulate an almost palpable sense of loss which laid claim to my life. A great gaping hole was blasted out of my world by the unexpected death of my father when I was nineteen years old. The way I learned to fill this hole, this void, was to write. My father taught me this as if to prepare me for his own passing. Writing allowed me direct access to my imagination, to inspiration and, ultimately, to God. I found that through the use of language I was writing God into existence. Language became the blanket that I threw over the invisible man, which gave him shape and form. The actualizing of God through the medium of the Love Song remains my prime motivation as an artist. I found that language became a poultice to the wounds incurred by the death of my father. Language became a salve to longing.

The loss of my father created in my life a vacuum, a space in which my words began to float and collect and find their purpose. The great W. H. Auden said, 'the so-called traumatic experience is not an accident, but the opportunity for which the child has been patiently waiting – had it not occurred, it would have found another – in order that its life become a serious matter.' The death of my father was the 'traumatic experience' Auden talks about which left the hole for God to fill. How beautiful the notion that we create our own personal catastrophes and that it is the creative forces within us that are instrumental in doing this. Here our creative impulses lie in ambush at the side of our lives, ready to leap forth and kick holes in it – holes through which inspiration can rise. We each have our need to create, and sorrow itself is a creative act.

Though the Love Song comes in many guises – songs of exaltation and praise, songs of rage and of despair, erotic songs, songs of abandonment and loss – they all address God, for it is the haunted premise of longing that the true Love Song inhabits. It is a howl in the void for love and for comfort, and it lives on the lips of the child crying for his mother. It is the song of the lover in need of their loved one, the raving of the lunatic supplicant petitioning his god. It is the cry of one chained to the earth and craving flight, a flight into inspiration and imagination and divinity.

The Love Song is the sound of our endeavours to become God-like, to rise up and above the earth-bound and the mediocre. I believe the Love Song to be a sad song. It is the noise of sorrow itself.

We all experience within us what the Portuguese call '*saudade*', which translates as an inexplicable longing, an unnamed and enigmatic yearning of the soul, and it is this feeling that lives in the realms of imagination and inspiration and is the breeding ground for the sad song, for the Love Song. '*Saudade*' is the desire to be transported from darkness into light, to be touched by the hand of that which is not of this world. The Love Song is the light of God, deep down, blasting up through our wounds.

In his brilliant lecture entitled 'The Theory and Function of Duende', Federico García Lorca attempts to shed some light on the eerie and inexplicable sadness that lives at the heart of certain works of art. 'All that has dark sounds has "*duende*",' he says, 'that mysterious power that everyone feels but no philosopher can explain.' In contemporary rock music, the area in which I operate, music seems less inclined to have at its soul, restless and quivering, the sadness that Lorca talks about.

Excitement, often; anger, sometimes – but true sadness, rarely. Bob Dylan has always had it. Leonard Cohen deals specifically with it. It pursues Van Morrison like a black dog and, though he tries to, he cannot escape it. Tom Waits and Neil Young can summon it. My friends The Dirty 3 have it by the bucket-load but, all in all, it would appear that '*duende*' is too fragile to survive the compulsive modernity of the music industry. In the hysterical technocracy of modern music, sorrow is sent to the back of the class, where it sits, pissing its pants in mortal terror. Sadness or '*duende*' needs space to breathe. Melancholy hates haste and floats in silence. I feel sorry for sadness, as we jump all over it, denying it its voice, and muscling it into the outer reaches. No wonder sorrow doesn't smile much. No wonder sadness is so sad.

All Love Songs must contain '*duende*' because the Love Song is never simply happy. It must first embrace the potential for pain. Those songs that speak of love, without having within their lines an ache or a sigh, are not Love Songs at all, but rather Hate Songs disguised as Love Songs and are not to be trusted. These songs deny us our human-ness and our God-given right to be sad, and the airwaves are littered with them. The Love Song must resonate with the whispers of sorrow and the echoes of grief. The writer who refuses to explore the darker regions of the heart will never be able to write convincingly about the wonder, the magic and the joy of love, for just as goodness cannot be trusted unless it has breathed the same air as evil – the enduring metaphor of Christ crucified between two criminals comes to mind here – so within the fabric of the Love Song, within its melody, its lyric, one must sense an acknowledgement of its capacity for suffering.

Sad Waters

Down the road I look and there runs Mary
Hair of gold and lips like cherries
We go down to the river where the willows weep
Take a naked root for a lovers' seat
That rose out of the bitten soil
But bound to the ground by creeping ivy coils
O Mary you have seduced my soul
Forever a hostage of your child's world

And then I ran my tin-cup heart along
The prison of her ribs
And with a toss of her curls
That little girl goes wading in
Rolling her dress up past her knee
Turning these waters into wine
Then she plaited all the willow vines

Mary in the shallows laughing
Over where the carp dart
Spooked by the new shadows that she cast
Across these sad waters and across my heart

Around the age of twenty, I started reading the Bible, and I found in the brutal prose of the Old Testament, in the feel of its words and its imagery, an endless source of inspiration, especially in the remarkable series of Love Songs/poems known as the Psalms. I found the Psalms, which deal directly with the relationship between man and God, teeming with all the clamorous desperation, longing, exhaltation, erotic violence and brutality that I could hope for. The Psalms are soaked in '*saudade*', drenched in '*duende*' and bathed in bloody-minded violence. In a lot of ways these songs became the blueprint for many of my more sadistic Love Songs. Psalm 137, a particular favourite of mine, which was turned into a chart hit by the fab little band Boney M, is a perfect example of this.

Psalm 137

By the rivers of Babylon, there we sat down, yea,
We wept, when we remembered Zion
We hanged our harps upon the willows in the midst thereof
For there they that carried us away captive required
Of us a song; and they that wasted us *required of us*
Mirth *saying,* Sing us *one* of the songs of Zion.
How shall we sing the Lord's song in a strange land?
If I forget thee, O Jerusalem. Let my right hand
Forget *her cunning.*
If I do not remember thee, let my tongue cleave to
The roof of my mouth: If I prefer not Jerusalem above my chief joy
Remember, O Lord, the children of Edom in the
Day of Jerusalem; who said Rase *it,* rase *it, even* to
The foundation thereof.
Daughter of Babylon, who art to be destroyed;
Happy *shall he be,* that rewardeth thee as thou hast
Served us.
Happy *shall he be,* that taketh and dasheth thy little
Ones against the stones.

Here, the poet finds himself captive in 'a strange land' and is forced to sing a song of Zion. He declares his love to his homeland and dreams of revenge. The psalm is ghastly in its violent sentiments, as he sings to his God for deliverance, and that he may be made happy by murdering the children of his enemies. What I found, time and time again in the Bible, especially in the Old Testament, was that verses of rapture, of ecstasy and love could hold within them apparently opposite sentiments – hate, revenge, bloody-mindedness, etc. – these sentiments were not mutually exclusive. This idea has left an enduring impression upon my song-writing.

The Love Song must be borne into the realm of the irrational, the absurd, the distracted, the melancholic, the obsessive and the insane, for the Love Song is the clamour of love itself, and love is, of course, a form of madness. Whether it is the love of God, or romantic erotic love – these are manifestations of our need to be torn away from the rational, to take leave of our senses, so to speak. Love Songs come in many forms and are written for a host of reasons, as declarations of love or revenge, to praise or to wound or to flatter – I have written songs for all these reasons – but ultimately the Love Song exists to fill, with language, the silence between ourselves and God, to decrease the distance between the temporal and the divine.

But, within the world of modern pop music, a world that deals ostensibly with the Love Song, true sorrow is just not welcome. Of course, there are exceptions, and occasionally a song comes along that hides behind its disposable plastic beat, a love lyric of truly devastating proportions. 'Better the Devil You Know', written by the hit-makers Stock, Aitken & Waterman and sung by the Australian pop sensation Kylie Minogue, is such a song. The disguising of the terror of love in a piece of mindless, innocuous pop music is an intriguing concept. 'Better the Devil You Know' contains one of pop music's most violent and distressing love lyrics.

Better the Devil You Know

Say you won't leave me no more
I'll take you back again
No more excuses, no, no
'Cause I've heard them all before
A hundred times or more
I'll forgive and forget

If you say you'll never go
'Cause it's true what they say
Better the devil you know

Our love wasn't perfect
I know, I think I know, the score
You say you love me, O boy
I can't ask for more
I'll come if you should call
I'll be here every day
Waiting for your love to show
'Cause it's true what they say
It's better the devil you know

I'll take you back
I'll take you back again

When Kylie Minogue sings these words there is an innocence to her voice that makes the horror of this chilling lyric all the more compelling. The idea presented within this song – dark and sinister and sad – that love relationships are by nature abusive, and this abuse, be it physical or psychological, is welcomed and encouraged, shows how even the most seemingly harmless of Love Songs has the potential to hide terrible human truths. Like Prometheus chained to his rock, the eagle eating his liver night after night, Kylie becomes Love's sacrificial lamb, bleating an earnest invitation to the drooling, ravenous wolf, to devour her time and time again, all to a groovy techno beat. 'I'll take you back. I'll take you back again.' Indeed. Here the Love Song becomes a vehicle for a harrowing portrait of humanity, not dissimilar to the Old Testament Psalms. Both are messages to God that cry out into the yawning void, in anguish and self-loathing, for deliverance.

As I said earlier, my artistic life has centred around the desire or, more accurately, the need, to articulate the various feelings of loss and longing that have whistled through my bones and hummed in my blood throughout my life. In the process I have written about 200 songs, the bulk of which I would say were Love Songs. Love Songs, and therefore, by my definition, sad songs. Out of this considerable mass of material, a handful of them rise above the others as true examples of all I have talked about. 'Sad Waters', 'Black Hair', 'I Let Love In', 'Deanna', 'From Her To Eternity', 'Nobody's Baby Now', 'Into My Arms', 'Lime Tree Arbour', 'Lucy', 'Straight To You'. I am proud of these songs. They are my gloomy, violent, dark-eyed children. They sit grimly on their own and do not play with the other songs. Mostly they were the offspring of complicated pregnancies and difficult and painful births. Most of them are rooted in direct personal experience and were conceived for a variety of reasons, but this rag-tag group of Love Songs are, at the death, all the same thing – lifelines thrown into the galaxies by a drowning man.

Here, ladies and gentlemen, is a new one.

Love Letter

I hold this letter in my hand
A plea, a petition, a kind of prayer
I hope it does as I have planned
Losing her again is more than I can bear
I kiss the cold, white envelope
I press my lips against her name
Two hundred words. We live in hope
The sky hangs heavy with rain

Love Letter Love Letter
Go get her Go get her
Love Letter Love Letter
Go tell her Go tell her

A wicked wind whips up the hill
A handful of hopeful words
I love her and I always will
The sky is ready to burst
Said something I did not mean to say
Said something I did not mean to say
Said something I did not mean to say
It all came out the wrong way

Love Letter Love Letter
Go get her Go get her
Love Letter Love Letter
Go tell her Go tell her

Rain your kisses down upon me
Rain your kisses down in storms
And for all who'll come before me
In your slowly fading forms
I'm going out of my mind
Will leave me standing in
The rain with a letter and a prayer
Whispered on the wind

Come back to me
Come back to me
O baby please come back to me

The reasons I feel compelled to write Love Songs are legion. Some of these became clearer to me when I sat down with a friend of mine who, for the sake of his anonymity, I will refer to as 'G'. 'G' and I admitted to each other that we both suffered from the psychological disorder that the medical profession terms 'Erotigraphomania'. Erotigraphomania is the obsessive desire to write Love Letters. 'G' shared with me the fact that he had written and sent, over the last five years, more than

7,000 Love Letters to his wife. My friend looked exhausted, and his shame was almost palpable. We discussed the power of the Love Letter and found that it was, not surprisingly, very similar to that of the Love Song. Both serve as extended meditations on one's beloved. Both serve to shorten the distance between the writer and the recipient. Both hold within them a permanence and power that the spoken word does not. Both are erotic exercises in themselves. Both have the potential to reinvent, through words, like Pygmalion with his self-created lover of stone, one's beloved. But more than that, both have the insidious power to imprison one's beloved, to bind their hands with love-lines, gag them, blind them, for words become the defining parameter that keeps the image of the loved one, imprisoned in a bondage of poetry. 'I have taken possession of you,' the Love Letter, the Love Song, whispers, 'for ever.' These stolen souls we set adrift like lost astronauts floating for eternity through the stratospheres of the divine. Me, I never trust a woman who writes letters, because I know that I myself cannot be trusted. Words endure, flesh does not. The poet will always have the upper hand. Me, I'm a soul-catcher for God. Here I come with my butterfly-net of words. Here I catch the chrysalis. Here I blow life into bodies and hurl them fluttering to the stars and the care of God.

I'd like to look finally at a song I wrote for the *Boatman's Call* album. It is called 'Far From Me', and I have a few things to tell you about it.

Far From Me

For you, dear, I was born
For you I was raised up
For you I've lived and for you I will die
For you I am dying now
You were my mad little lover
In a world where everybody fucks everybody else over

You who are so
Far from me
So far from me
Way across some cold neurotic sea
Far from me

I would talk to you of all manner of things
With a smile you would reply
Then the sun would leave your pretty face
And you'd retreat from the front of your eyes
I keep hearing that you're doing your best
I hope your heart beats happy in your infant breast
You are so far from me
Far from me
Far from me

There is no knowledge but I know it
There's nothing to learn from that vacant voice
That sails to me across the line
From the ridiculous to the sublime
It's good to hear you're doing so well
But really, can't you find somebody else that you can ring and
  tell?
Did you ever care for me?
Were you ever there for me?
So far from me

You told me you'd stick by me
Through the thick and through the thin
Those were your very words
My fair-weather friend
You were my brave-hearted lover
At the first taste of trouble went running back to mother
So far from me
Far from me

Suspended in your bleak and fishless sea
Far from me
Far from me

'Far From Me' took four months to write, which was the duration of the relationship it describes.

The first verse was written in the first week of the affair and is full of all the heroic drama of new love, describing the totality of feeling whilst acknowledging its parallel pain – 'for you I'm dying now.' It sets the two lover-heroes against an uncaring world – 'a world that fucks everybody over' – and brings in the notion of the physical distance suggested in the title. Verse one, and all is well in the garden. But the thing is, 'Far From Me' had its own agenda and was not about to allow itself to be told what to do. The song, as if awaiting the inevitable 'traumatic experience', simply refused to let itself be completed until the catastrophe had occurred. Some songs are tricky like that, and it is wise to keep your wits about you when dealing with them. I find more often than not that the songs I write seem to know more about what's going on in my life than I do. I have pages and pages of final verses for this song, written while the relationship was still sailing happily along. One such verse went:

The Camellia, the Magnolia
Have such a pretty flower
And the bell from St Mary's
Informs us of the hour

Pretty words, innocent words, unaware that any day the bottom was about to drop out of the whole thing. As I wrote the final verse of 'Far From Me' it became clear that my life was being dictated by the largely destructive ordinance of the song itself, that it had its own inbuilt destiny, over which I had no control. In fact, I was an afterthought, a bit-part player in its sly, mischievous and finally malicious vision of how the world should be.

Love Songs that attach themselves to actual experience, which are a poeticizing of real events, have a beauty unto themselves. They stay alive in the same way that memories do and, being alive, they grow up and undergo changes and develop. If a song is too weak to do that, if it is lacking in sufficient stamina and the will to endure, sadly, it will not survive. You'll come home one day and find it dead in the bottom of its cage. Its soul will have been reclaimed and all that will remain is a pile of useless words. A Love Song such as 'Far From Me' demanded a personality beyond the one I originally gave it, with the power to influence my own feelings and thoughts around the actual event itself. The songs that I have written that deal with past relationships have become the relationships themselves, heroically mutating with time and mythologizing the ordinary events of my life, lifting them from the temporal plane and blasting them way into the stars. As the relationship itself collapses, whimpering with exhaustion, the song breaks free of it and beats its wings heavenward. Such is the singular beauty of song-writing.

Twenty years of song-writing have now passed, and still the void gapes wide. Still the inexplicable sadness, the '*duende*', the '*saudade*', the divine discontent, persists, and perhaps it will continue until I see the face of God himself. But when Moses desired to see the face of God, he was answered that he may not endure it, that no man could see the face of God and live. Well, me, I don't mind. I'm happy to be sad. For the residue, cast off in this search, the songs themselves, my crooked brood of sad-eyed children, rally round and, in their way, protect me, comfort me and keep me alive. They are the companions of the soul that lead it into exile, that sate the overpowering yearning for that which is not of this world. The imagination demands an alternate world and through the writing of the Love Song one sits and dines with loss and longing, madness and melancholy, ecstasy, magic and joy with equal measure of respect and gratitude.

'The Secret Life of the Love Song' was delivered as a lecture at the South Bank Centre, London, in 1999

A Note on the Albums

A list of songs is given at the beginning of each album in this book. Where a list is divided into two parts, the latter section refers to songs written around the same period as the album but which were used as either B-sides to singles, or in other projects.

Nick Cave and The Bad Seeds released a collection called *B-sides and Rarities* in 2005. There is, however, no separate section for this album. The lyrics to these songs are published here according to the period in which they were written.

Prayers on Fire
(1981)

Zoo-Music Girl
Cry
Nick the Stripper
Figure of Fun
King Ink
A Dead Song
Yard
Just You and Me

Release the Bats
Mr Clarinet
Happy Birthday
The Friend Catcher
Kathy's Kisses

Zoo-Music Girl

Zoo-Music Girl Zoo-Music Girl
Our life together is a hollow tooth
Spit out the shells, spit out the shells
You know exactly what I'm talking about
Don't drag the orchestra into this thing
Rattle those sticks, rattle those sticks
The sound is beautiful, it's perfect!
The sound of her young legs in stockings
The rhythm of her walk, it's beautiful
Just let it twist, let it break
Let it buckle, let it bend
I want the noise of my Zoo-Music Girl
Zoo-Music Girl, Zoo-Music Girl
My body is a monster driven insane
My Heart is a fish toasted by flames
I kiss the hem of her skirt
We spend our lives in a box full of dirt
I murder her dress till it hurts
I murder her dress and she loves it
If there is one thing I desire in the world
Is to make love to my Zoo-Music Girl
Zoo-Music Girl Zoo-Music Girl
The sound is beautiful! It's perfect!
I call out her name in the night
Zoo-Music Girl! Zoo-Music Girl!
I call her by her family name
Zoo-Music Girl! Zoo-Music Girl!
Oh! God! Please let me die beneath her fists
Zoo-Music Girl! Zoo-Music Girl!
Zoo-Music Girl! Zoo-Music Girl!

Cry

When you walk outa here
When you walk out
I gotta fill up that space
Or fill up that no-space
I'll fill it up with tears
I'll fill it up with tears
I'll fill it up with tears
I'll fill it up with tears
Cry Cry Cry Cry
Where no fish can swim
Where no fish can swim
Where no-fish can swim
Where no-fish can
Cry Cry Cry

When you slam that door
When that door slams
I gotta fill up that space
And I'll pack my suitcase
I'll fill it up with clothes
Or fill it up with no-clothes
And I'll pack it up with tears

I'll pack it up with tears
Cry Cry Cry Cry
Where no fish can swim
Where no fish can swim
Where no-fish can swim
Cry Cry Cry

When you say goodbye
When you say goodbye
I'll dig myself a hole
And fill up that space
I'll fill it up with flesh
And I'll fill it up with no-flesh
I'll fill it up with tears
I'll fill it up with tears

Fish Swim Cry Fish Crryyy

Nick the Stripper

Nick the Stripper
Hideous to the eye
Hideous to the eye
He's a fat little insect
A fat little insect
And OOOOOOOOOH! here we go again

Nick the Stripper
Dances on all fours
Dances on all fours
He's in his birthday suit
He's in his birthday suit
and OOOOOOOOOH! here we go again

Nick the Stripper
Hideous to the eye
Hideous to the eye
He's a fat little insect
A fucked little insect
and OOOOOOOOOH! here we go again
Insect Insect Insect Insect

Figure of Fun

I am a figure of fun
Dead-pan and moribund
All the things I do are better left undone
I am a figure of fun

And I bake in the sun
I have no luck in Love
I have no luck in anything
I am a figure of fun

And I'm impressed by everyone
But I impress no one
It's irritating
I am a figure of fun

I am a figure of fun
I have money
But money isn't everything to a figure of
Fun fun fun fun fun fun

King Ink

King Ink strolls into town
He sniffs around

King Ink kicks off his stink-boot
Sand and soot and dust and dirt and
He's much bigger than you think
King Ink
King Ink, wake up, get up
Wake up, up, up, up, up, up
A bug crawls up the wall
King Ink feels like a bug
And he hates his rotten shell
Cha-cha-cha-cha-cha-cha-cha-cha
King Ink, get up, go forth
Wake up – what's in that room?
Wake up – what's in that house?
Express thyself, say something loudly
AAAAAAAH! What's in that room?
Sand and soot and dust and dirt
King Ink feels like a bug
Swimming in a soup-bowl
Oh! Yeah! Oh! Yeah! What a wonderful life
Fats Domino on the radio

A Dead Song (with Anita Lane)

(*This is true*)
Mister nothing said forever said
I can sing
Hit it! Make it a dead one
With words like
Blood, soldier, mother
OK OK
I want to sleep before the end
Which is impolite
Hit it! Make it a dead one
If nothing crops up
I'll give you a ring
You can sing the end
OK OK
Then I could get
All the little animals out of my room
Hit it! With a broom
OK OK
Put them in a big white sack
No visitors came
Hit it! WITH WORDS LIKE . . .
Thou shalt not
The End

Yard

In our yard
How many chickens can we count
On our fingers and toes
On their toes
Sitting on father's hole
Sitting on his chest
Crushing rocks of dirt
The earth is soft in our
Yard Yard
Stones in my shoes
And feet
Dragging them through museums
Where
Under glass
Refrigerate
Freeze
Hands and feet
And knobbly knees
Yard Yard

Just You and Me

First: I tried to kill it with a hammer
Thought that I could lose the head
Sure! We've eaten off the silver
(When even food was against us)
And then I tried to kill it in the bed
Second: I gagged it with a pillow
But awoke the nuns inside my head
They pounded their Goddy-Goddy fists
(From the inside – so from the outside)
I got good: I stuck it. Dead
Thirdly: I put my lips upon it
And blew a frost across its flat
I wrote upon its outside-surface
'Tonite we're on the outside-surface'
Just you and me girl: you and me and the fat

Release the Bats

Whooah Bite! Whooah Bite!
Release the bats! Release the bats!
Don't tell me that it doesn't hurt
A hundred fluttering in your skirt
Don't tell me that it doesn't hurt

My baby is all right
She doesn't mind a bit of dirt
She says 'Horror vampire bat bite'
She says 'Horror vampire
How I wish those bats would bite'
Whoooah Bite! Bite!

Release the bats! Release the bats!
Pump them up and explode the things
Her legs are chafed by sticky wings
(Sticky sticky little things)

My baby is a cool machine
She moves to the pulse of her generator
Says damn that sex supreme
She says damn that horror bat
Sex vampire, cool machine

Release the bats! Release the bats!

Baby is a cool machine
She moves to the pulse of a generator
She says damn that sex supreme

She says, she says damn that horror bat
Sex horror sex bat sex horror sex vampire
Sex bat horror vampire sex
Cool machine
Horror bat. Bite!
Cool machine. Bite!
Sex vampire. Bite!

Mr Clarinet

I have a friend in you, oh Mr Clarinet
You make me laugh, and then cry like the song of the clarinet
Marry me, marry me alive O
I put on my coat of trumpets
Will she be there? Is my piccolo on straight?

Her white stockings and red dress that goes
swish, swish swish around her legs of lace

Marry me, marry me alive O

Could you tell her
Would you tell her for me, oh Mr Clarinet
That I love her love her, oh love her
I love her but I cannot wait

Marry me, marry me alive O

I love her, love her, love her
Love her love her love her love her

Happy Birthday

It's a very happy day
We had lots of fun fun fun
And it's ice-cream and jelly
and a punch in the belly
How much can you throw over the walls?

And see how his face glows
It's a bike! What a surprise
It's a big bike. What a big surprise
It's a red bike. What a red surprise
Oh, what a surprise

But the best thing there
But the best thing there
Was the wonderful dog chair
Was the beautiful dog chair
That could count right up to ten
It could count right up to ten
It went woof, woof, woof, woof, woof
woof, woof, woof, woof, woof

And it's another happy day
He was born eleven years ago
And this year it's long trousers
and a very smart tie
Just think in five years he'll be shaving

And see how his face glows
It's a bike. What a surprise!
It's a samurai sword
What a metal surprise
He'll remember this day for the rest of his life

But the best thing there
But the best thing there
Is that fabulous dog chair
The immaculate dog chair
That could count right up to eleven
It could count right up to eleven
It went woof, woof, woof, woof, woof, woof
woof, woof, woof, woof, woof, woof

But the best thing there
But the best thing there
Was my darling the dog chair
But the rampaging dog chair
That could count right up to eleven
It could count right up to eleven

And it went round and round the house

The Friend Catcher

I: cigarette fingers
Puff and poke, puff and poke
And the smoke it touches the ground

You: your lungs in your wrists
They throb like trains
Choo choo choo choo
It's a prison of sound

See by the hair of my chinny-chin-chin
Hee-haw! Hee-haw! Hee-haw!
I can't see for smoke
So I poke around

I poke around

Kathy's Kisses

Kathy's kisses, they fall out of
Her mouth on to the floor, collect dust
I sweep them under the door

Junkyard
(1982)

Big–Jesus–Trash–Can
Kiss Me Black
6'' Gold Blade
Kewpie Doll
Junkyard
She's Hit
Dead Joe
Hamlet (Pow, Pow, Pow)

Sometimes Pleasure Heads Must Burn

Big–Jesus–Trash–Can

Big–Jesus soul-mates trash–can
fucking rotten business this
both feet in the Bad-Boot
stiff in the crypt, baby, like a rock
rock-rock-rock
Big–Jesus soul-mates trash–can
pumped me fulla trash at least it smelt like trash
wears a suit of Gold (got greasy hair)
but God gave me Sex appeal

well-well-well-well-rock
well-well-well-well-rock
well-well-well-well-rock
well-well-well-well-rock
he drives a trash–can
he drives a trash–can
he drives a trash–can
he drives a trash–can
he's comin' to my town rock-rock-rock-
r-o-o-o-o-o-o-o-o-o-o-o-o-o-o-o-o-ck!

Big–Jesus–oil–King down in Texas
drives great holy tanks of Gold
Screams from heaven's Graveyard
American heads will roll in Texas
(roll like Daddies' Meat)
roll under those singing stars of Texas

well-well-well-well-rock
well-well-well-well-rock
well-well-well-well-rock
well-well-well-well-rock

he drives a trash–can
he drives a trash–can
he drives a trash–can
he drives a trash–can
He's comin' to my town, He's comin' to my town
He's comin' to my town, He's comin' to my town

Kiss Me Black

Now they put the stink on us
Throw us to the succubus
Fed us to the incubus
And brung in the Saprophagous
c'mon and kiss me black
I need to feel your lips around me
c'mon and kiss me black
Black as the pit in which you found me

She's like a dog you have to kick her
Sleeps like a swastika
And says 'everyone's a winner now
cos everyone's a sinner now'
come on and kiss me black
come and sail your ships around me
c'mon and kiss me black
Black as the sea in which you drowned me

C'mon and kiss me black
Run your rusty cutlass through me
C'mon and kiss me black
Kiss me black and then undo me

6'' Gold Blade

I stuck a six-inch gold blade in the head of a girl
She lying through her teeth, him: on his back
Hands off this one, hands off! she cried
Grinning at me from hip to hip
Hands off, pretty baby, tough bone then so soft to slip
Oooh Yeah
I stuck a six-inch gold blade in the head of a girl
Shark's-fin slices sugar-bed slices that pretty red-head
I love you! now me! I love you!
Laughter, laughter
Oh baby, those skinny girls, they're so quick to murder
Oooh Yeah
Shake it baby, c'mon, shake, shake it baby
Shake
Shake
Shake
Shake

Kewpie Doll

Well I love that kewpie doll
Well I love that kewpie doll
Well I love that kewpie doll
Yeah I bought her in a show
I dressed her up in a cheap red cotton dress
But everything was either fished–out or spat–out
Fished–out or spat–out
Well I love that kewpie doll
But I could not make it stick
Well I love that kewpie doll
But I could not make it stick
Only she could save my soul
She put her hands inside of me
Well I love that kewpie doll
Dressed her in a cheap-red-cotton-dress
Fished it out now spat it out now
Spat it out in front of me
Well I love that kewpie doll
But I could not make it stick
Doll doll doll doll doll doll doll doll
I held her in my cheap arms
She believed in me, she believed in me
Her soul and my arms
Well I love that kewpie doll
I told her phoney stories
Well I love that kewpie doll
She believed in me
Doll doll doll doll doll doll doll doll
Kewpie on a stick
I can see her coming even now
Kewpie on a stick
I can see her walking to me even now

Well I love that kewpie doll
I can see her walking to me even now
Well I love that kewpie doll
I can see her walking to me even now
Well I love that kewpie doll
But I could not make it stick.

Junkyard

I am the King. I am the King. I am the King

One dead marine through the hatch
Scratch and scrape this heavenly body
Every inch of winning skin
There's garbage in honey's sack again

Honey Honey Honey Honey Honey
Come on and kiss me
Honey Honey Honey Honey Honey
Honey-child's taking over this place

Two dead marines standing in a line
Drink to me! this heavenly body
Every inch a winning thing

Honey Honey Honey Honey Honey
Come on and kiss me
Honey Honey Honey Honey Honey
Honey-child's taking over this place

Hack hack hack hack this heavenly
Yack yack yack yack yack goes junk-face
Scratch scrape scratch this winning skin
There's garbage in Honey's sack again
There's garbage in Honey's sack again
There's garbage in Honey's sack again
Garbage in honey Garbage in honey
Junkyard King Junkyard King
King King King King King

She's Hit

there is woman-pie in here
mr evangelist says she's hit
the best cook you ever had
you can't blame the good-woman now, dad
and you locked him up for twenty years
now there's action on the basement stairs
a monster half-man half-beast
hear the hatchet (grind grind)
pilgrim gets 1 hacked daughter
and all we guys get are forty hack reporters
uptown one hundred skirts are bleeding
mr evangelist says
she's hit ev'ry little bit
she's hit ev'ry little bit
now if only we could all grow wings and fly
sweet hatchet swing low son
I'm feeling pretty lonesome
christen the bastard jack dad
the head-shrinker is a quack
'anyone who'd wear their hair like that'
the vinyl is so cool, the conversation's cruel
hold my heart romeo it's in a rodeo
hold my head daddy-o it just won't go
and all the girls across the world
and all the girls across the world
are hit ev'ry little bit

Dead Joe

oh-ho-ho-ho-ho-ho-ho-ho-ho-ho Dead Joe
oh-ho-ho-ho-ho-ho-ho-ho-ho-ho Dead Joe

welcome to the car smash
welcome to the car smash
welcome to the car smash
Dead Joe

Junk-Sculpture turning back to junk
Junk-Sculpture turning back to junk
Junk-Sculpture turning back to junk
Dead Joe
oh joe n-o-o-o-o-o! it's christmas time Joe
it's christmas time now for you
and all the little bells are hanging two-by-two
the holly and the nativity
oh speak to me Joe speak to me Joe speak to me oh
oh-oh-oh---oh--oh--oh--oh--oh--oh--oh
De-e-e-e-e-e-e-e-e-e-e-e-e-e-ead Joe

oh-ho-ho-ho-ho-ho-ho-ho-ho-ho Dead Joe
oh-ho-ho-ho-ho-ho-ho-ho-ho-ho Dead Joe

welcome to the car smash
welcome to the car smash
welcome to the car smash
you can't tell the girls from the boys anymore
you can't tell the girls from the boys anymore
you can't tell the girls from the boys anymore
Oh-oh-oh-oh-oh-oh---oh--oh--oh---oh---oh---oh
De-e-e-e-e-e-e-e-e-e-e-e-e-e-ead Joe

Hamlet (Pow, Pow, Pow)

Hamlet's fishin' in the grave
Hamlet's fishin' in the grave
thru the custard bones and stuff
he ain't got no friends in there
he ain't got no friends in there
I believe our man's in love
Hamlet got a gun now
he wears a crucifix
he wears a crucifix
pow pow pow pow/pow pow pow pow
Hamlet moves so beautiful
Hamlet moves so beautiful
walking thru the flowers
who are hiding 'round the corners
He's movin' down the street now
he likes the look of that cadillac
he likes the look of that cadillac
pow pow pow pow/pow pow pow pow
Is this love some kinda love
Is this love some kinda love
Now he's movin' down my street
and he's coming to my house
crawling up my stairs
Wherefore art thou baby-face
Where-for-art-thou
pow pow pow pow/pow pow pow pow
Is this love
Is this love
Pow!
He shoot it inside
He shoot it inside

Pow!
Don’t let ’em steal your heart away
he went and stole my heart POW!!
hey hey hey POW!!

Sometimes Pleasure Heads Must Burn

BU-U-U-U-U-U-U-RN! POP! POP!
BU-U-U-U-U-U-U-RN! POP! POP!
I reckon I'm a bit too close to this one
I reckon if I touch it might just burn
Flesh-heads like me just wax and melt
When my tongue touches titty's tongue in turn
Sometimes pleasure heads must
BU-U-U-U-U-U-U-RN! POP! POP!
BU-U-U-U-U-U-U-RN! POP! POP!
My brain tricked my hands to believe they were strong
In short, my hands became clubs to grind
I reckon I'm a bit too close to this one
Kiss me darling, kiss my eyes to blind
Kiss my clubs and witness what my knuckles find
BU-U-U-U-U-U-U-RN! POP! POP!
BU-U-U-U-U-U-U-RN! POP! POP!
I feel a little low, you know what I mean?
Buried neck-high in British snow
I reckon I'm a bit too close to this one
Shoot me darling, shoot me in the head and go
Ya! Ya! Teeth gone. Follow my trail back home
Ya! Ya! Teeth gone. Follow my trail back home
Ya! Ya! BU-U-U-U-U-U-U-RN! POP! POP!

The Bad Seed
(1983)

Sonny's Burning
Wild World
Fears of Gun
Deep in the Woods

Sonny's Burning

Have you heard how Sonny's burning
Like some bright erotic star?
He lights up the proceedings
And raises the temperature
Flame on! Flame on!

Now I've seen to Sonny's Burning
Someday I think I'll cut him down
But it can get so cold in here
And he gives off such an evil heat
Flame on! Flame on!
Hail my incubatic incubator

Now pay witness to Sonny's Burning
Warming the damp and rotten seed
Warming the damp and rotten seed
That blooms into the demon flower
Now fire and flowers both consume me
Flame on! Flame on!

Evil heat is running through me
Flame on! Flame on!
Sonny's burning pits into me
Flame on! Flame on!
Sonny's burning holes into me
Don't interrupt! Don't interrupt!
Flame on! Flame on!

Wild World

Hold me up baby for I may fall
Hold my dish-rag body tall
Our bodies melt together (we are one)
Post crucifixion baby, and all undone

It's a wild world

Church bells ring out the toll of our night
Forward and forever backward
Forever backward forever forward all right
Strophe and antistrophe
Strophe and antistrophe
(C'mon baby, hold me tight)
It's a wild world, a wild world
Up here in your arms tonight

Don't push me
Don't push me

It's a wild world

Fears of Gun

Gun wears his alcoholism well
Finger in Bottle and swingin' it still
From Bed to Sink and back again
Clock is crawlin' round the same
He's bustin' Clock (he hates its face)
Just sittin' and talkin' to Heart in ticks
Talkin' back to Clock in slow and studied kicks
The fears of Gun are the fears of everyone

Fingers down the throat of love
Fingers down the throat of love
Fingers down the throat of love
Love! Love!

Gun does the waltz around the room
Collecting Table and Chairs and Sofa and so on and so on
Gun wears his best blue suit, now let's take to the sky
'We'll go dancin' and eatin' it up
Get a bottle and push it on down'
And let's just beat it up
Transistor radio plays an overwhelmingly sad and lonely song
Saying 'Where she gone? Where she gone?'
The fears of Gun are the fears of everyone

Fingers down the throat of love
Fingers down the throat of love
Love! Love!

Deep in the Woods

The woods eats the woman and dumps her honey-body in the mud
Her dress floats down the well and it assumes the shape of the body of a little girl
Yeah I recognize that girl
She stumbled in some time last loneliness
But I could not stand to touch her now
My one and onlyness

Deep in the woods
Deep in the woods
Deep in the woods a funeral is swinging

Worms make their cruel design
Saying D-I-E into her skin
Saying DEAD into belly and DEATH into shoulder
Well last night she kissed me but then death was upon her

Deep in the woods
Deep in the woods
Deep in the woods a funeral is swinging

Now the killed waits for the killer
And the trees all nod their heads, they are agreed
This knife feels like a knife feels like a knife that feels like it's feed
Yeah I recognize that girl
I took her from rags right through to stitches
Oh baby, tonight we sleep in separate ditches

Deep in the woods
Deep in the woods
Deep in the woods a funeral is swinging

Love is for fools and all fools are lovers
It's raining on my house and none of the others
Love is for fools and God knows I'm still one
The sidewalks are full of love's lonely children
The sidewalk regrets that we had to kill them

Burning the Ice
(The Die Haut Album, 1983)

Truck Love
Stow-A-Way
Dumb Europe
Pleasure is the Boss

Truck Love

Truck love! Right here!
Truck love! Right now!
Bewitched by pure power. That's truck love!
In the gully of your choice. Truck love!
Jam-up on a leaping tree. Head on! Head first!
And God came down and talked to me
And I damn nearly wept
Tears rolling down the dash! Tears rolling down the dash!
We can't stop the monster rolling
We can't stop the monster rolling
We can't stop the monster rolling
We can't stop the monster rolling
Rise to power! Rise to power!
Rise to power! Rise to power!
Your eyes stare bright like gold
Eye-spot interference all across the fucking road
Burn my eyes! Burn my eyes! Baby!
My hands keep shaking when I'm touching ya
My hands keep shaking when I'm touching ya
They keep shaking when I ain't
They keep shaking when I ain't

Truck love! Truck love!
Pit-stop lovers!
Right now and the now is right!
This highway is done bent on killing us
Testing every nerve that we possess between us
The face of Christ is leaping from the storm
The face of Christ is leaping from the storm
You tend to get religious on these runs
Rise to power! Rise to power!
Rise to power! Rise to power!

Divine power has gone crawled into this tank
Every metal muscle flexed and pumping at the crank
Pumping at my axis. Rendering me sexless
Mega-tons of muscle kicking dust across Texas
Truck love! Out on the city limits
Drive straight into the eye of the next town that we hit
Gun it once for the hillbillies
Just to make them shit

Fuck love! This truck love!
Fuck love! This truck love!
The dolls on the grille are caked in bloody bug guts
The dolls on the grille are caked in bloody bug guts
Truck love! Truck love!
Rise to power! Rise to power!
The dolls on the grille are caked in bloody bug guts
The dolls on the grille are caked in bloody bug guts
Truck love! Truck love!
There are things burning in the desert
Rise to power! Rise to power!
There are things burning in the desert
Rise to power! Rise to power!
There are things burning in the desert

Stow-A-Way

Hey hey I am the stow-a-way
Hey hey I am the stow-a-way

My girl turned as blue as an iceberg do
And me I'm totally shipwrecked over her
Baby baby don't blow away
Hey hey I am the stow-a-way
I am the stow-a-way

This is your captain talking to ya
This is your captain talking to ya
This is your captain talking to ya
This is your captain talking to ya

Heartache

Hey hey I am the stow-a-way
I am the stow-a-way

My baby turned as blue as an iceberg do
And I sank to the bottom of the sea
Hey baby don't blow away
Hey hey I am the stow-a-way
I am the stow-a-way

This is your doctor talking to ya
This is your doctor talking to ya
This is your doctor talking to ya
This is your doctor talking to ya

Heartache

Dumb Europe

On this European night out on the brink
The cafés and the bars still stink
The air is much too thick for seeing
But not thick enough for leaning
I leave in a catatonic crawl
And if I die tonight then throw me in
Some bleak teutonic hole
Six feet under with a snap-frozen soul
And really we could all just die of shame
And really we could all just die of shame
Dumb Europe, Dumb Europe, Dumb Europe

Oh the Utopian night on the brink
Mama's face staring up at me from the bottom of the sink
Witness my trail of destruction
Trying to leave this drinking place
My feet are magnetized for furniture
The floor's attracted to my face
And if I die tonight
Sell me as some prehistoric bone
A lump of junk-souvenir for Jap
To fob off on his friends back home
The money-dance . . .
I find it hard to cope with days like this. Pass the bottle
Dumb Europe, Dumb Europe, Dumb Europe

On this European night out on the brink
The cafés and the bars still stink
The air is much too thick for seeing
But not thick enough for leaning

I leave in a catatonic crawl
And if I die tonight then throw me in
Some bleak teutonic hole
Six feet under with a snap-frozen soul
And really we could all just die of shame
And really we could all just die of shame
Dumb Europe, Dumb Europe, Dumb Europe

Pleasure is the Boss

They're working us like dogs around here
'Cause pleasure is the boss
And I'm the happiest slave alive around here
'Cause pleasure is the boss
And nothing is safe that don't stand still
If it's OK with the boss
I'm gunna walk right up and take it yeah
If it's OK with the boss

Walk!

What's OK with the boss is OK with me
What's OK with the boss is OK with me

What's OK with the boss is OK with me
What's OK with the boss is OK with me

What's OK with the boss is OK with me
What's OK with the boss is OK with me

Mutiny!
(1983)

Jennifer's Veil
Mutiny in Heaven
Swampland

Vixo

Jennifer's Veil

So you've come back for Jennifer
You know, she hides her face behind a veil
I'm warning you Frankie, leave on the next train
Your Jennifer she just ain't the same
Quit waving that thing about! Come back!
Come back and give me a chance to explain
Your baby will never cry again

So don't try to reach out
And don't let the ship's flag down
Point the figure-head at the storm
And drive her hard upon
Don't stop and don't stop
And don't let the veil drop
(Another ship ready to sail – the rigging is tight
Tight like Jennifer's veil)

She drew the curtain on her face
Ever since they came and burnt the old place down
Why is she searching through the ashes?
Why, only Jennifer knows that now
And the officer, without a word
Left all his junk and just moved out

So don't try to reach out
And don't let the ship's flag down
Point the figure-head at the glass
Smash! Smash! Into shards
Don't stop and don't touch!
And don't let the veil drop . . . behind Jennifer's veil

Oh God! Frankie! Is that really you!
Get back! Don't reach out!
Get back, and get that lantern out of my room!

Don't try to reach out
And don't let the ship's flag down
Down, down over her, like a shroud
And let her sail on the sea like a stone
Don't touch and don't touch
And don't let the veil drop
Another ship ready to dock . . . the rigging comes loose . . .
Loose like Jennifer's veil

Mutiny in Heaven

Well ah jumpt! and fled this fucken heap on doctored wings
Mah flailin pinions, with splints and rags and crutches!
(Damn things nearly hardly flap)
Canker upon canker upon one million tiny punctures
That look like . . .
Long thin red ribbons draped across the arms of a lil mortal girl
(Like a ground-plan of Hell)
Curse these smartin strings! These fucken ruptures!
Enough! Enough is enough!
(If this is Heaven ah'm bailin out)
If this is Heaven, ah'm bailin out!
Ah caint tolerate this ol tin-tub
So fulla trash and rats! Felt one crawl across mah soul
For a seckon there, ah thought ah wassa back down in the ghetto!
(Rats in Paradise! Rats in Paradise!)
Ah'm bailin out! There's a mutiny in Heaven!

Ah wassa born . . .
And Lord shakin, even then was dumpt into some icy font
like some great stinky unclean!
From slum-church to slum-church, ah spilt mah heart
To some fat cunt behind a screen . . .
Evil poppin eye presst up to the opening
He'd slide shut the lil perforated hatch . . . at night mah body blusht
To the whistle of the birch
With a lil practice ah soon learnt to use it on mahself
Punishment?! Reward!! Punishment?! Reward!!
Well, ah tied on . . . percht on mah bed ah was . . .
sticken a needle in mah arm . . .

Ah tied off! Fucken wings burst out mah back
(Like ah was cuttin teeth!!)
Ah took off!!!
(Rats in Paradise! Rats in Paradise!)
There's a mutiny in Heaven!

Oh Lord, ah git down on mah knees
(Ah git down on mah knees and start to pray)
Wrapt in mah mongrel wings, ah nearly freeze
In the howlin wind and drivin rain
(All the trash blowin round 'n' round)
From slum-heaven into town
Ah take mah tiny pain and rollin back mah sleeve
(Roll anna roll anna roll anna roll)
Ah yank the drip outa mah vein! UTOPIATE! Ah'm bailin out!
UTOPIATE!
If this is Heaven ah'm bailin out!
Mah threadbare soul teems with vermin and louse
Thought comes like a plague to the head . . . in God's house!
Mutiny in Heaven!
(Ars infectio forco Dio)
To the plank!
(Rats in Paradise! Rats in Paradise!)
Ah'm bailin out!
(Hail Hypuss Dermio Vita Rex!)
Hole inna ghetto! Hole inna ghetto!
(Scabio Murem per Sanctum . . . Dio, Dio, Dio)

Swampland

Quixanne, ah'm in its grip
Quixanne, ah'm in its grip
Sinken in the mud
Patron-saint of the Bog
They cum with boots of blud
With pitchfawk and with club
Chantin out mah name
Got doggies strainin onna chain
Lucy, ah'll love ya till the end!
They hunt me like a dog
Down in Sw-a-a-a-amp Land!

So cum mah executioners! Cum bounty hunters!
Cum mah county killers – for ah cannot run no more
Ah cannot run no more
Ah cannot run no more
No I can't!
Lucy, ya won't see this face agin
When ya caught ya swing and burn . . .
Down in Sw-a-a-a-amp Land!

The trees are veiled in fog
The trees are veiled in fog
Like so many jilted brides
Now they're all breakin down and cry
Cryin tears upon mah face
Cryin tears upon mah face
And they smell of gasoline
a-a-a-a-ah scr-e-e-e-a-am
Lucy, ya made a sinner out of me
Now ah'm burnin like a saint
Down in Sw-a-a-a-amp Land!

So cum mah executioners! Cum mah bounty huntahs!
Cum mah county killers – ya know ah cannot run no more
No ah cannot run no more

Vixo

Ah fed Vixo on every fear 'n' fret 'n' phobia
Til it nor ah could stand the strain no longer
Sucked a chicken-bone, tossed it in the corner
Raisin up like Lazarus, up, up from its cot
An making for the door, now . . .
Infant-prodigy creates a phantom-friend, yeah
Stickin' sack an ol' Jack-Jack into its itchin-ten
Oh! Don't ya linger! Ooh! Don't ya linger, now
Mah monster-piece . . . mah perfect-murder-machine
Don't ya linger, for ah can feel mah youth slipping outa me
Yeah, ah can feel mah youth slip outa me

Call it, Call it Vixo. Call it Vee
Ah all it, an it comes to me
Call it Vixo. Call it me
March headlong into the heart of fear
Ah will follow thee

What kept ya? Whaa? What kept ya? You get trouble? Sum'n
go wrong?
Vixo grinning, climbs up into mah lil boy arms
What you get? Tell me, what ya gone 'n' brung me from the
hollow?
Yeah! We're laughin' . . . but our laughter is shallow
Ain't it funny . . . my childhood name is Sorrow
Vixo sighs, 'n' lays its head upon mah pillow

Call it. Call it Vixo. Call it Vee
Call it, an it comes to me
Vee . . . ah . . . Hex . . . Oh-oh, come crawl with me
Into the dark heart of despair
Ah will not forsake thee

Listen . . . Instruction!
Ditch it, Pitch it. Now hitch it up along the ridge
Ya laughin b'neath the Sheriff's wheels
That go screamin cross Hooper Bridge
Skirt the out-skirts. Up mah back-stair. Ya sack all undone
Don't touch nothin! Water runnin in the tub
Get there! and scrub ev'ry one

When ya STRUCK ya struck a thousand crickets dumb
Hooper-Hollow iced over then, all hush, hush
In the cool midday sun
Hush! Ah say Hush! Hu-u-u-ush!
Sittin on the roof, laugh at mahself
As they rope off the woods
Watchin all the good-people
go beating the bush

From Her to Eternity (1984)

Cabin Fever!
Well of Misery
From Her to Eternity
Saint Huck
Wings off Flies
A Box for Black Paul

The Moon is in the Gutter
Just a Closer Walk with Thee
The Six Strings that Drew Blood
Oh I Love You Much Too Much

Cabin Fever!

The Captain's fore-arm like buncht-up rope
With A-N-I-T-A wrigglin free outa skull 'n' dagger
And a portrait of Christ, nailed to an anchor
Etched into the upper . . .
Slams his fucken tin dish down
Our Captain takes time to crush
Some bloo-bottles glowin in his gruel
With a lump in his throat and lumpy mush
Thumbing a scrap-book stuck up with clag
And a morbid lump of love in his flags
Done is the kissing, now all that remains
Is to sail for ever upon the stain
Cabin Fever! O, O O Cabin Fever!
The Captain's free hand is a cleaver
With which he fashions his beard and rations his jerky
And carves his peg outa the finest mahogany!
Or was it ebony? Yeah, it was ebony!
He tallies up his loneliness notch by notch
For the sea offers nuthin to hold or touch
Notch by notch, winter by winter
Notch by notch, winter by winter
Now his leg is whittled right down to a splinter
O, O Cabin Fever! Cabin Fever!
O the rollin sea still rollin on!
She's everywhere! now that she's gone! Gone! Gone!
O Cabin Fever! O Cabin Fever!

Welcome to the table, his belovéd-unconscious
Raisin her nest of hair from her crooks
And strugglin to summon up one of her looks!

His arm now, like coiled s-s-s-snakes
Whips all the bottles that he's drunken
Like crystal skittles about the cabin
Of a ship they'd been sailing five years sunken

Well of Misery

Along crags and sunless cracks I go
Up rib of rock, down spine of stone
I dare not slumber where the night winds whistle
Lest her creeping soul clutch this heart of thistle

O the same God that abandoned her
Has in turn abandoned me
And softening the turf with my tears
I dug a well of misery

And in that well of misery
Hangs a bucket full of sorrow
Which swings slow and aching like a bell
Its toll is dead and hollow

Down that well lies the long-lost dress
Of my little floating girl
That muffles a tear that you let fall
All down the well of misery

Put your shoulder to the handle if you dare
And hoist that bucket hither
Crank and hoist and hoist and crank
'Til your muscles waste and wither

O the same God that abandoned her
Has in turn abandoned me
Deep in the Desert of Despair
I wait at the Well of Misery

From Her to Eternity

Ah wanna tell ya bout a girl
You know, she lives in Room 29
Why that's the one right up top a mine
Ah start to cry, ah start to cry-y
O ah hear her walkin
Walkin barefoot cross the floor-boards
All through this lonesome night
And ah hear her crying too
Hot tears come splashin down
Leakin through the cracks
Down upon my face, ah catch em in my mouth!
Walk 'n' Cry, Walk 'n' Cry-y!!
From her to eternity
From her to eternity
From her to eternity
Ah read her diary on her sheets
Scrutinizin evry lil piece of dirt
Tore out a page 'n' stufft if inside my shirt
Fled outa the window
And shinning it down the vine
Outa her nightmare and back into mine
Mine! O mine!
From her to eternity
From her to eternity
From her to eternity
Cry! Cry! Cry!
She's wearin them bloo-stockens, ah bet!
And standin like this with my ear to the ceiling
Listen ah know it must sound absurd
But ah can hear the most melancholy sound
Ah ever heard!

Walk 'n' Cry! Kneel 'n' Cry-y!
From her to eternity
From her to eternity

O tell me why? why? why?
Why the ceiling still shakes?
Why the furniture turns to serpents 'n' snakes?
This desire to possess her is a wound
And it's naggin at me like a shrew
But ah know that to possess her
Is therefore not to desire her
O, O, O then ya know, that lil girl would just have to go!
Go! Go-o-o! From her to eternity

Saint Huck

Born of the river
Born of its never-changing, ever-changing murky water
Old river-boat keeps rolling along
Through the great grey greasy city
Huck standing like a saint upon its deck
If ya wanna catch a saint
Then bait ya hook. Let's take a walk . . .

'O come to me! O come to me!' is what the dirty city
Say to Huck
He go woah-woah, woah woah!
Saint Huck! Huck!

Straight into the arms of the city go Huck
Down the beckonin streets of opportunity
Huck whistles his favourite river-song . . .
And a bad-bline-nigger at the piano
Puts a sinister-bloo-lilt to that sing-a-long
Huck senses something's wrong!!
Sirens wail in the city
And lil-Ulysses turn to putty
Ol man River's got a bone to pick!
Our boy's hardly got a bone to suck!
He goa woah-whoa, woah woah!
Saint Huck! Huck!

The moon, its huge cycloptic eye
Watches the city streets contract
Watchem twist and cripple and crack
Saint Huck goes on a dog's leg now
Saint Huck goes on a dog's leg now

Why, you know the story!
Ya wake up one morning and ya find you're a thug
Cracking ya knuckles in some dive
Ya fingers hot and itchin, blowin smoke rings
Ya bull-neck bristlin . . .
Still Huck he ventures on whistlin
And Death reckons Huckleberry's time is up
O woah woah woah woah!
Saint Huck! Huck!

Yonder go Huck, minus pocket-watch an' wallet gone
Skin shrink-wraps his skeleton
No wonder he git thinner, wot with his cold 'n' skinny dinners!
Saint Huck-a-Saint Elvis, Saint Huck-a-Saint Elvis
O you remember the song ya used to sing-a-long
Shifting the river-trade on that ol' steamer
Life is just a dream!
But ya traded in the mighty ol' man River
For the dirty ol man Latrine!
The brothel shift
The hustle 'n' the bustle and the green-back's rustle
And all the sexy cash
And the randy cars
And the two dollar fucks
O, O O ya outa luck, outa luck
Woah-woah-woah-woah
Saint Huck! Huck!

These are the tracks of deception
They lead to the heart of despair
Huck whistles like he just don't care
That in the pocket of the jacket is a chamber
And a lead pellet sleeps in there
Wake up!
Huck whistles and he kneels and he lays down there

See ya Huck. Good luck!
A smoke ring hovers above his head
And the rats and the dogs and the men all come
And put a bullet through his eye
And the drip and the drip and the drip of the Mississippi
crying
And Saint Huck hears his own Mississippi just rolling by him
He goes, he goes woah-woah-woah, woah-woah-woah!
Saint Huck! Saint Huck!
Saint Huck! Saint Huck!

Wings off Flies

She loves me, she loves me not
She loves me, she loves me not

Well I've spent seven days and seven nights
Trying to get sunk in this brine
Don't turn on your water-works
'Cause I've got me a pair of water-wings, right?!
Insects suicide against the window
And my heart goes out to those little flies
There's a buzzing in my ear
But it's more of her blackmail, ham Shakespeare and lies
Wings off flies
She loves me, she loves me not
O, O O O oh she loves me not!

Lord, I've discovered the recipe of Heaven
You get solitude and mix with sanctuary and silence
Then bake it!
Listen, I plead guilty to misanthropy
So hang me! I'd appreciate it!
Witness her gate-crash my tiny hell
With some obscene tête-à-tête
If you want to talk to me about love and pain
Consult my ulcer, it'd be happy to co-operate
Wings off flies
She loves me, she loves me not
Hey Joe, another ought to do the job

Time to drown our little fire, you can keep the ashes
Now bye bye, bye bye, see you in a pig's eye!
I will be one, in need of no one
In this, my deepest dive . . .

Fill her up, Joe . . .
Hey! I am obliged! I am obliged!
Wings off flies
She loves me, she loves me not

A Box for Black Paul

Who'll build a box for Black Paul?
I'm enquiring on behalf of his soul
I'd be beholden to you all
For a little information, just some kind of indication
Just who will dig the hole

When you've done ransacking his room
Grabbing anything that shines
Throw the scraps down on the street
Like all his books and his notes
All his books and his notes and all the junk that he wrote
The whole fucking lot right up in smoke
Ain't there nothing sacred anymore?
Who will build a box for Black Paul?

And they're shooting off his guns
And they're shooting off their mouths
Saying 'Fuck with us . . . and die!'
(But see that rat of fear go scuttle in their skulls)
'Cover that eye!' 'Cover that frozen eye!'
Black puppet, in a heap up against the stoning-wall
Blood puppet go to sleep, Mama won't scold you anymore
Armies of ants wade up the little red streams
Heading for the mother-pool
O Lord it's cruel! O man it's hot!
And some of those ants they just clot to the spot
Who cast the first stone at Black Paul?

'Don't ask us,' say the critics and the hacks
The pen-pushers and the quacks
'We jes cum to git dah facks!!'
'We jes cum to git dah facks!!'

Here is the hammer that built the scaffold
And built the box,
Here is the shovel that dug the hole
In this ground of rocks
And here is the pile of stones!
And for each one planted, God only knows
A blood-rose grown . . .

These are the *true* Demon-Flowers!
These are the *true* Demon-Flowers!
Stand back everyone! Blood-black every one!

Who'll build a box for Black Paul?
Who'll carry it up the hill?

'Not I,' said the widow, adjusting her veil
'Ah will not drive the nail
Or cart his puppet-body home
For ah done that one thousand times before
Yeah! ah done that one thousand times or more
And why should ah dress his wounds
When he has wounded my dress, nightly
Right across the floor?'

Who'll build a box for Black Paul?
And who'll carry it up the hill?
Who'll bury him in the black soil?

From the woods and the thickets
Come the ghosts of his victims
'We love you!'
'*I* love you!'
And 'This won't hurt a bit,

We'll go up, up, up, up, up into Death
Up, up, up, up. Inhale its breath!
Oh O, Death favours those that favour Death'

Here is the stone, and this is the inscription that it bears:
'Below Lies Black Paul, Under The Upper
But Above And Beyond The Surface-Flat-Fall There'

And all the angels come on down
And all the men and women crowd around
And all the widows weeping into their skirts
And all the little girls and the little boys
And all the scribes with pens poised
And all the hullaballoo, and all the noise
All the hallaballoo, all the noise
All the hallaballoo and all of the noise

Black Paul clears his throat of black blood
And sings in the voice of a lonely boy . . .

> Well I have cried one thousand tears
> I've cried a thousand tears, it's true
> And the next stormy night you know
> That I'm still crying them for you
>
> Well I had a girl she was so sweet
> Red dress, and long red hair hanging down
> And heaven just ain't heaven
> Without that little girl hanging around
>
> Well you know I've been a bad man
> And Lord knows I've done some good things too
> But I confess, my soul will never rest
> Until you, until you build
> Until you build a box for my girl too

The Moon is in the Gutter

The moon is in the gutter
And the stars wash down the sink
I am the king of the blues
I scrape the clay off my shoes
And wade down the gutter and the moon

The moon blinds my eye with opal cataracts
As I cut through the saw-mills and the stacks
Leaping over the gully where I would one day take Lucy
Then wash up my hands in the gully and the moon

The moon is in the gutter
All my plans are flushed down the drain
I wonder lonely as a cloud
Over memories at her mound
Then lie down in the bitter gutter moon

Just a Closer Walk with Thee

Just a closer walk with thee
Come back, honey, to me
Then I'll be moving up close to thee
O let it be, O Lord, let it be

I go to the garden all alone
Deception lurking at every turn
If to have that rose I must hold the thorn
Then let it be, O Lord, let it be

Love's sweet garden overgrown
Gone is the rose and deep is the thorn
If I must walk these paths alone
Then let it be, please Lord, on up to thee

The Six Strings that Drew Blood

Guitar thug blew into town
His eyes like wheels spinnin' round
And jerkin' off at every sound
Layin' all his crosses down
He got six strings
The six strings that drew blood
He got six strings
Six strings that drew blood

The bar is full of holy Joes
Holy holy ho-leerio
Round the neck of our consumptive rose
Is the root of all his sorrow
He got six strings
Six strings that drew blood

Holy holy ho-leerio
Holy holy ho-leerio
Holy holy ho-leerio
Six strings that drew blood

In the bathroom under cover
He turns on one tap to discover
That he's smashed his teeth out on the other
And he says to the mirror 'Hey don't fuck me brother
'cause I've got six strings'
Yeah six strings that drew blood

With the runt of reputation they call rat fame
Top E as a tourniquet
A low tune whistles across his grave
Forever the master and the slave
Of his six strings

Holy holy ho-leerio
Holy holy ho-leerio
Holy holy ho-leerio
Six strings that drew blood

Oh I Love You Much Too Much

Oh I love you much too much
Slow-talking pain
comes on like a rolling grub
Smothers like a snail's foot
Would a tiny lady bug
Robs my yellow garden bright
Of its spring-time sunshine breath
Hairy stalk, pod, bud, seed, bead
Loving bee, gnome, elf, self: Death

The First-Born is Dead (1985)

Tupelo
Say Goodbye to the Little Girl Tree
Train Long-Suffering
Black Crow King
Knockin' On Joe
Wanted Man
Blind Lemon Jefferson

Scum

Tupelo

Looka yonder!
Looka yonder!
Looka yonder!
A big black cloud come!
O comes to Tupelo. Comes to Tupelo

Yonder on the horizon
Stopped at the mighty river and
Sucked the damn thing dry
Tupelo-o-o, O Tupelo
In a valley hides a town called Tupelo

Distant thunder rumble
Rumble hungry like the Beast
The Beast it cometh, cometh down
Wo wo wo-o-o, Tupelo bound
Tupelo-o-o, yeah Tupelo
The Beast it cometh, Tupelo bound

Why the hen won't lay no egg
Cain't get that crock to crow
The nag is spooked and crazy
O God help Tupelo, O God help Tupelo!

Ya can say these streets are rivers
Ya can call these rivers streets
Ya can tell yaself ya dreaming buddy
But no sleep runs this deep
Women at their windows
Rain crashing on the pane

Writing in the frost Tupelo's shame
Tupelo's shame
O God help Tupelo! O God help Tupelo!

O go to sleep lil children
The sandman's on his way
O go to sleep lil children
The sandman's on his way
But the lil children know
They listen to the beating of their blood
They listen to the beating of their blood
The sandman's mud!
The sandman's mud!
And the black rain come down
Water water everywhere
Where no bird can fly no fish can swim
No fish can swim
Until the King is born!
Until the King is born!
In Tupelo! Tupelo-o-o!
Til the King is born in Tupelo!

In a clap-board shack with a roof of tin
Where the rain came down and leaked within
A young mother frozen on a concrete floor
With a bottle and a box and a cradle of straw
Tupelo-o-o! O Tupelo!
With a bundle and a box and a cradle of straw

Well Saturday gives what Sunday steals
And a child is born on his brother's heels
Come Sunday morn the first-born's dead
In a shoe-box tied with a ribbon of red
Tupelo-o-o! Hey Tupelo!
In a shoe-box tied with a ribbon of red

O mama rock your lil one slow
O ma-ma rock your baby
O ma-ma rock your lil one slow
O God help Tupelo! O God help Tupelo!
Mama rock your lil one slow
The lil one will walk on Tupelo
Tupelo-o-o! Yeah Tupelo!
And carry the burden of Tupelo
Tupelo-o-o! O Tupelo!
Yeah! The King will walk on Tupelo
Tupelo-o-o! O Tupelo!
He carried the burden of Tupelo!
Tupelo-o-o! Hey Tupelo!
You will reap just what you sow

Say Goodbye to the Little Girl Tree

O say goodbye to the little girl tree
O you know that I must say goodbye
To the little girl tree
This wall I built around you
Is made out of stone lies
O little girl the truth would be
An axe in thee
O father look to your daughter
Brick of grief and stricken mortar
With this ring, this silver hoop of wire
I bind your maiden mainstem
Just to keep you as a child

O say goodbye to the little girl tree
O you know that I must say goodbye
To my little girl tree
How fast your candy bones
Reached out for me
I must say goodbye to your brittle bones
Crying out for me
O you know that I must say goodbye
O goodbye
Even though you will betray me
The very minute that I leave

O say goodbye to the little girl tree
O Lord you know that I must say goodbye
To that little girl tree
I rise up her girl-child lumps and slipping knots
Into her laden boughs
And amongst her roping limbs
Like a swollen neck-vein branching

Into smaller lesser veins
That must all just sing and say goodbye
And let her blossom veils fly
Her velvet gown
Down down down
Down down down
Down down down – and goodbye
For you know that I must say goodbye

To a rhythm softly tortured
Of a motion back and forth
That's a rhythm sweetly tortured
O that's the rhythms of the orchard
And you know that I must say goodbye
To that little girl tree
O goodbye. Yes goodbye
For you know that I must die
Down down down
Down down down
Down down down and goodbye
For you know that I must die
Yes you know that I must die
O you know that I must die

Train Long-Suffering

Woo-woooooooooo Woo!
In the name of pain!
  (In the name of pain and suffering)
In the name of pain!
  (In the name of pain and suffering)
There comes a train
  (There comes a train)
Yeah! A long black train
  (There comes a train)
Lord, a long black train

Woo-woo! woo-woo!

Punched from the tunnel
  (The tunnel of love is long and lonely)
Engines steaming like a fist
  (A fistful of memories)
Into the jolly jaw of morning
  (Yeah! O yeah!)
O baby it gets smashed!
  (You know that it gets smashed)
O baby it gets smashed!
  (You know that it gets smashed)

I kick every goddam splinter
Into all the looking eyes in the world
Into all the laughing eyes
Of all the girls in the world
Ooooooo-wooooooh
She ain't never coming back
She ain't never coming back
She ain't never coming back

And the name of the pain is . . .
The name of the pain is . . .
The name of the pain is
A train long-suffering

On rails of pain
 (On rails of pain and suffering)
There comes a train
 (There comes a train long-suffering)
On rails of pain
 (On rails of pain and suffering)
O baby blow its whistle in the rain

Woo-oo Woo! Woo-woo Woo!

Who's the engine-driver?
 (The engine-driver's over yonder)
His name is Memory
 (Memory is his name)
O Memory is his name
 (Wooooooo-oo!)
Destination . . . Misery
 (Pain and misery)
O pain and misery
 (Pain and misery)
O pain and misery! Hey! Hey!
 (Pain and misery)
Hey! that's a sad looking sack!
Oooh that's a sad looking sack!
And the name of the pain is . . .
And the name of the pain is . . .
Oooh the name of the pain is . . .
A train long-suffering

There is a train!
  (It's got a name)
Yeah! It's a train long-suffering
O Lord a train
  (A long black train)
Lord! Of pain and suffering
Each night so black
  (O yeah! So black)
And in the darkness of my sack
I'm missing you baby
  (I'm missing you)
And I just don't know what to do
  (Don't know what to do)
  (Train long-suffering, Train long-suffering)
Train long-suffering. Train long-suffering
O she ain't never coming back
O she ain't never coming back
O she ain't never coming back
O she ain't never coming back
And the name of the pain is . . .
The name of the pain is . . .
The name of the train is . . .
The name of the train is
Pain and suffering

Black Crow King

Mmmmm Mmmmmm Mmmmm
I am the black crow king
Mmmmmmm Mmmmm Mmmmmmm
I am the black crow king
Keeper of the nodding corn
Bam! Bam! Bam! Bam!
All the hammers are a-talking
All the nails are a-singing
So sweet and low

You can hear it in the valley
Where live the lame and the blind
They climb the hill out of its belly
They leave with mean black boots on

'I just made a simple gesture
They jumped up and nailed it to my shadow
My gesture was a hooker
You know, my shadow's made of timber'

And this storm is a-rolling
And this storm is a-rolling
All down on me

And I'm still here rolling after everybody's gone
And I'm still here rolling after everybody's gone
I'm still here rolling and I'm left on my own
The blackbirds have all flown!
Everyone's rolled on!

I am the black crow king
Keeper of the trodden corn
I am the black crow king
I won't say it again
And the rain it raineth daily, Lord
And wash away my clothes
I surrender up my arms
To a company of crows

I am the black crow king
I won't say it again
And all the thorns are a-crowning
Ruby on each spine
And the spears are a-sailing
O my o my

And the storm is a-rolling
The storm is a-rolling
All down on me

And I'm still here rolling after everybody's gone
I'm still here rolling after everybody's gone
I'm still here rolling and left on my own
Those blackbirds they have flown and I am on my own

I am the black crow king
Keeper of the forgotten corn
The King! The King!
I'm the king of nothing at all
The hammers are a-talking
The nails are a-singing
The thorns are a-crowning him
The spears are a-sailing
The crows are a-mocking
The corn is a-nodding

The storm is a-rolling
The storm is a-rolling
The storm is a-rolling
The storm is a-rolling
The storm is a-rolling
Down on me
Rolling down on me
Rolling down on me

Knockin' On Joe

These chains of sorrow, they are heavy, it is true
And these locks cannot be broken, no, not with one thousand keys
O Jailor, you wear a ball-and-chain you cannot see
You can lay your burden on me
You can lay your burden down on me
You can lay your burden down upon me
But you cannot lay down those memories

Woooo wooo wooo
Woooo wooo wooo
Here I go!
Knockin' on Joe!
This square foot of sky will be mine till I die
Knockin' on Joe
Woooo wooo wooo
All down the row
Knockin' on Joe

O Warden I surrender to you
Your fists can't hurt me anymore
You know, these hands will never wash
These dirty Death Row floors
O Preacher, come closer, you don't scare me anymore
Just tell Nancy not to come here
Just tell her not to come here anymore
Tell Nancy not to come
And let me die in the memory of her arms

O Wooo wooo wooo
Wooo wooo woooo
All down the row
Knockin' on Joe

O you kings of halls and ends of halls
You will die within these walls
And I'll go, all down the row
Knockin' on Joe

O Nancy's body is a coffin, she wears my tombstone at her head
O Nancy's body is a coffin, she wears my tombstone at her head
She wears her body like a coffin
She wears a dress of gold and red
She wears a dress of gold and red
She wears a dress of red and gold
Grave-looters at my coffin before my body's even cold

It's a door for when I go
Knockin' on Joe
These hands will never mop your dirty Death Row floors
No! You can hide! You can run!
O but your trial is yet to come
O you can run! You can hide!
But you have yet to be tried!
You can lay your burden down here
You can lay your burden down here
Knockin' on Joe
You can lay your burden upon me
You can lay your burden down upon me
Knockin' on Joe
You can't hurt me anymore
Knockin' on Joe

Wanted Man

I'm a wanted man
Wanted man
I'm wanted
I'm a wanted man
O yeah, O honey I'm a wanted man

....
....
....
....

....
....
....
....

....
....

Wanted man in Arizona, wanted man in Galveston
Wanted man in El Dorado, this wanted man's in great
demand

If you ever catch me sleeping
And you see a price flash above my head
Take a look again my friend, that's a gun pointing at your head
....
....

Wanted man by the Borland sisters, wanted man by Kate
Callaghan
Honey don't you try and tell me you don't want me
'Cause I'm a wanted man

Wanted man who's lost his will to live
wanted man who won't lay down
There's a woman kneeling at an unmarked grave
Pushing daisies in the ground

Wanted man in the windy city, wanted man in Tennessee
Wanted man in Broken Arrow, wanted man in Wounded Knee
Wanted man in Jackson town, wanted man in El Paso
I've got bounties on my head in towns I would never think to go

Wanted man in Arizona, wanted man in Louisville
Wanted man deep in Death Valley
Wanted man up in the Hollywood hills

If the Devil comes collecting
'Cause heaven don't want no wanted man
He'd better wear a six-gun on his hip and hold another in his
hand

If you love a wanted man, you'd best hold him while you can
Because you're going to wake up one morning
and find the man you wanted he is gone

Wanted man in New York City, wanted man in San Antone
Wanted man down in Lorado, wanted man in Tupelo

Wanted man in the state of Texas, wanted man in the state of
Maine
This wanted man's in the state of leaving you baby
jumping on that midnight train

Wanted man in every cat-house, wanted man in a million
saloons
Wanted man is a ghost in a hundred houses
a shadow in a thousand rooms

Wanted man down at St Louis, wanted man in New Orleans
Wanted man in Muscle Bay, wanted man in Cripple Creek
Wanted man in Detroit City, wanted man in San Antone
But there's one place I'm not wanted, Lord
it's the place that I call home

O wanted man, wanted man
If the Devil comes collecting he'd better hold a six-gun in his
hand

Blind Lemon Jefferson

Bline Lemon Jefferson is a-comin
Tap tap tappin with his cane
Bline Lemon Jefferson is a-comin
Tap tap tappin with his cane
His last ditch lies down the road of trials
Half filled with rain

O sycamore, sycamore!
Stretch your arms across the storm
Down fly two greasy brother crows
They hop n bop n hop n bop hop on bop
Like the tax-man to come to call
They go knock knock! knock knock!
Hop n bop hop n bop
They slap a death-writ on his door

Here come the Judgement train
Git on board!
And turn that big black engine home
O let's roll! Let's roll!
Down the tunnel
The terrible tunnel of his world
Waiting at his final station
Like a bigger blacker third bird
O let's roll! Let's roll!

O his road is dark and lonely
He don't drive no Cadilac
O his road is dark and holy
He don't drive no Cadilac
If that sky serves as his eyes
Then that moon is a cataract

Let's roll! Yeah let's roll!

Scum

Well, I lived with one
Well, I lived with one
I lived with two
I even lived with a third
I wanna tell you about number one
He was a miserable shitwringing turd
Like he reminded me of some evil gnome
Shakin' hands was like shakin' a hot, fat, oily bone
Holdin' on for far too long
Yes, he took me in, he took me in
He said that I looked pale and thin
I told him he looked fat
His lips were red and lickin' wet
His house was roastin' hot
In fact it was a fuckin' slum
Scum!
Scum!
Well, then he hooked up with some slut from the same game
Black snow!
Black snow!
Cocksuckstress, and I should know
Mean and vicious, her microphone always smelled suspicious
His and herpes bath towel type
If you know what I mean
I could not look at him, worm
He'd be takin a shower and who should walk in
He was the epitome of their type
Her middle name was Welcome, his was Wipe
Scum!
Scum!
Well, you're on the shit list
Thrust and twist, twist and screw

You gave me a bad review
And maybe you think that it's all just water under the bridge
Well, my Unfriend, I'm the type that holds a grudge
I'm your creator
I think you fuckin' traitor, chronic masturbator
Shitlicker, user, self-abuser, jigger jigger!
What rock did you crawl from?
Which meathorse did you come?
You Judas, Brutus, Vitus
Scum!
Hey, four-eyes, come
That's right, it's a gun
Face bubbles blood in Grub street
Snowman with six holes clean into his fat fuckin' guts
Psychotic drama mounts
Guts well deep then spring abounds
I unload into his eyes
Blood springs
Dead snow
Blue skies

Your Funeral, My Trial
(1986)

Sad Waters
The Carny
Your Funeral, My Trial
Jack's Shadow
Hard on for Love
She Fell Away

God's Hotel

Sad Waters

Down the road I look and there runs Mary
Hair of gold and lips like cherries
We go down to the river where the willows weep
Take a naked root for a lovers' seat
That rose out of the bitten soil
But bound to the ground by creeping ivy coils
O Mary you have seduced my soul
Forever a hostage of your child's world

And then I ran my tin-cup heart along
The prison of her ribs
And with a toss of her curls
That little girl goes wading in
Rolling her dress up past her knee
Turning these waters into wine
Then she plaited all the willow vines

Mary in the shallows laughing
Over where the carp dart
Spooked by the new shadows that she cast
Across these sad waters and across my heart

The Carny

And no one saw the carny go
And the weeks flew by
Until they moved on the show
Leaving his caravan behind
It was parked up on the south-east ridge
And as the company crossed the bridge
With the first rain filling the bone-dry river bed
It shone, just so, upon the edge

Dog-boy, Atlas, Half-man, The Geeks, the hired hands
There was not one among them that did not cast an eye
behind
In the hope that the carny would return to his own kind

And the carny had a horse, all skin and bone
A bow-backed nag that he named Sorrow
Now it is buried in a shallow grave
In the then parched meadow

And the dwarfs were given the task of digging the ditch
And laying the nag's carcass in the ground
And Boss Bellini, waving his smoking pistol around
Saying 'The nag is dead meat
We can't afford to carry dead weight'
The whole company standing about
Not making a sound
And turning to the dwarfs perched on the enclosure gate
The Boss says 'Bury this lump of crow bait'

And then the rain came hammering down
Everybody running for their wagons
Tying all the canvas flaps down

The mangy cats growling in their cages
The Bird-Girl flapping and squawking around

The whole valley reeking of wet beast
Wet beast and rotten hay
Freak and brute creation
Packed up and on their way
The three dwarfs peering from their wagon's hind
Moses says to Noah 'We shoulda dugga deepa one'
Their grizzled faces like dying moons
Still dirty from the digging done

And as the company passed from the valley
Into higher ground
The rain beat on the ridge and on the meadow
And on the mound
Until nothing was left, nothing at all
Except the body of Sorrow
That rose in time
To float upon the surface of the eaten soil

And a murder of crows did circle round
First one, then the others flapping blackly down

And the carny's van still sat upon the edge
Tilting slowly as the firm ground turned to sludge

And the rain it hammered down

And no one saw the carny go
I say it's funny how things go

Your Funeral, My Trial

I am a crooked man
And I've walked a crooked mile
Night, the shameless widow
Doffed her weeds, in a pile
The stars all winked at me
They shamed a child
Your funeral, my trial

A thousand Marys lured me
To feathered beds and fields of clover
Bird with crooked wing cast
Its wicked shadow over
A bauble moon did mock
And trinket stars did smile
Your funeral, my trial

Here I am, little lamb . . .
Let all the bells in whoredom ring
All the crooked bitches that she was
(Mongers of pain)
Saw the moon
Become a fang
Your funeral, my trial

Jack's Shadow

They dragged Jack and his shadow
From the hole
And the bulb that burned above him
Did shine both day and night
And his shadow learned to love his
Little darks and greater light
And the sun it shined
And the sun it shined
And the sun it shined
A little stronger

Jack wept and kissed his shadow
'Goodbye'
Spat from the dirty dungeons
Into a truly different din
Shat from their institutions
Into a fully different din
And his shadow soon became a wife
And children plagued his latter life
Until one night he took a skinning knife
And stole into the town
And tracked his shadow down

Said that shadow to Jack Henry
'What's wrong?'
Jack said 'A home is not a hole
And shadow you're just a gallow that I hang my body from
O shadow you're a shackle from which my time is never done'
Then he peeled his shadow off in strips
He peeled his shadow off in strips
Then he kneeled his shadow on some steps
And cried 'what have I done?'

And the sun it shined
And the sun it shined
I say 'Love is blind'
And is it any wonder?
Is it any wonder?
Jack and his damned shadow
Is gone
And though each one of us are want to duly mourn
And though each one of us are want to duly mourn
'Tis done in brighter corners now
'Tis done in brighter corners now
Now that Jack's black shadow's gone

And the sun it shines
And the sun it shines
And the sun it shines
A little stronger

I swear, love is blind
Oooh love is blind
Yeah love is blind
And is it any wonder?

'Tis done in brighter corners now
'Tis done in brighter corners now
Now that Jack's black shadow's gone

Hard on for Love

It is for she that the cherry bleeds
That the moon is steeped in milk and blood
That I steal like a robber
From her altar of love
O money lender! O cloven gender!
I am the fiend hid in her skirts
And it's as hot as hell in here
Coming at her as I am from above
Hard on for love. Hard on for love
Hard on for love. Hard on for love

Well, I swear I seen that girl before
Like she walked straight outa the book of Leviticus
But they can stone me with stones I don't care
Just as long as I can get to kiss
Those gypsy lips! Gypsy lips!
My aim is to hit this Miss
And I'm movin in (I'm moving in)
Comin at her like Lazarus from above
Hard on for love. Hard on for love
Hard on for love. Hard on for love

The Lord is my shepherd I shall not want
The Lord is my shepherd I shall not want
But he leadeth me like a lamb to the lips
Of the mouth of the valley of the shadow of death
I am his rod and his staff
I am his sceptre and shaft
And she is Heaven and Hell
At whose gates I ain't been delivered

I'm gunna give them gates a shove
Hard on for love. Hard on for love
Hard on for love. Hard on for love

And her breasts rise and fall
Her breasts rise and fall
Her breasts rise and fall
Her breasts rise and fall

And just when I'm about to get my hands on her
Just when I'm about to get my hands on her
Just when I'm about to get my hands on her
Just when I'm about to get my hands on her
You are beautiful! O dove!
Hard on for love. Hard on for love
Hard on for love. Hard on for love

Just when I'm about to get my hands on her
Just when I'm about to get my hands on her

Her breasts rise and fall
Her breasts rise and fall

Just when I'm about to get my hands on her
Just when I'm about to get my hands on her

Hard on for love. Hard on for love
Hard on for love. Hard on for love

She Fell Away

Once she lay open like a road
Carved apart the madness that I stumbled from
But she fell away
She fell away
Shed me like a skin
She fell away
Left me holding everything

Once the road lay open like a girl
And we drank and laughed and threw the bottle over
But she fell away
She fell away
I did not see the cracks form
As I knelt to pray
I did not see the crevice yawn, no

Sometimes
At night I feel the end it is at hand
My pistol going crazy in my hand
For she fell away
O she fell away
Walked me to the brink
Then fell away
I did not see her fall
To better days
Sometimes I wonder was she ever there at all
She fell away
She fell away
She fell away

God's Hotel

Everybody got a room
Everybody got a room
Everybody got a room
In God's Hotel
Everybody got a room
Well you'll never see a sign hangin on the door
Sayin 'No vacancies here anymore'

Everybody got wings
Everybody got wings
Everybody got wings
In God's Hotel
Everybody got wings
You'll never see a sign hangin on the door
Sayin 'At no time may both feet leave the floor'

Everybody got a harp
Everybody got a harp
Everybody got a harp
In God's Hotel
Everybody has got a harp
You'll never see a sign hangin on the wall
Sayin 'No harps allowed in the hotel *at all*'

Everybody got a cloud
Everybody got a cloud
Everybody got a cloud
In God's Hotel
Everybody got a cloud
Well you'll never see a sign hangin in the hall
Sayin 'Smoking and drinking will be thy downfall'

Everybody holds a hand
Everybody holds a hand
Everybody holds a hand
In God's Hotel
Everybody holds a hand
You'll never see a sign hung up above your door
'No visitors allowed in rooms, *By Law!*'

Everybody's halo shines
Everybody's halo shines
Everybody's halo shines
In God's Hotel
Everybody's halo lookin fine
You won't see a sign staring at you from the wall
Sayin 'Lights Out! No burnin the midnight oil!'

Everybody got credit
Everybody got credit
Everybody got credit
In God's Hotel
Everybody got good credit
You'll never see a sign stuck on the cash-box drawer
Sayin 'Credit Tomorrow!!' or 'Want Credit?!? Haw, haw haw!!'

Everybody is blind
Everybody is blind
Everybody is blind
In God's Hotel
Everybody is blind
You'll never see a sign on the front door
'No red-skins. No Blacks. And that means you, baw!'

Everybody is deaf
Everybody is deaf
Everybody is deaf

In God's Hotel
Everybody is deaf
You'll never find a sign peeling off the bar-room wall
'Though shalt not blaspheme, cuss, holler or bawl'

Everybody is dumb
Everybody is dumb
Everybody is dumb
In God's Hotel
Everybody is dumb
So you'll never see on the visiting-room wall
'Though shalt not blaspheme, cuss, holler or bawl'

Tender Prey
(1988)

The Mercy Seat
Up Jumped the Devil
Deanna
Watching Alice
Mercy
City of Refuge
Slowly Goes the Night
Sunday's Slave
Sugar Sugar Sugar
New Morning

Girl at the Bottom of My Glass
That's What Jazz is to Me

The Mercy Seat

It began when they come took me from my home
And put me in Dead Row
Of which I am nearly wholly innocent you know
And I'll say it again
I . . . am . . . not . . . afraid . . . to . . . die

I began to warm and chill
To objects and their fields
A ragged cup, a twisted mop
The face of Jesus in my soup
Those sinister dinner deals
The meal trolley's wicked wheels
A hooked bone rising from my food
All things either good or ungood

And the mercy seat is waiting
And I think my head is burning
And in a way I'm yearning
To be done with all this measuring of truth
An eye for an eye
A tooth for a tooth
And anyway I told the truth
And I'm not afraid to die

Interpret signs and catalogue
A blackened tooth, a scarlet fog
The walls are bad, black, bottom kind
They are the sick breath at my hind
They are the sick breath at my hind
They are the sick breath at my hind
They are the sick breath gathering at my hind

I hear stories from the chamber
How Christ was born into a manger
And like some ragged stranger
Died upon the cross
And might I say it seems so fitting in its way
He was a carpenter by trade
Or at least that's what I'm told

My good hand tattooed E.V.I.L.
Across its brother's fist
That filthy five! They did nothing to challenge or resist

In Heaven His throne is made of gold
The ark of His testament is stowed
A throne from which I'm told
All history does unfold
Down here it's made of wood and wire
And my body is on fire
And God is never far away

Into the mercy seat I climb
My head is shaved, my head is wired
And like a moth that tries
To enter the bright eye
I go shuffling out of life
Just to hide in death awhile
And anyway I never lied

My kill-hand is called E.V.I.L.
Wears a wedding band that's G.O.O.D.
'Tis a long-suffering shackle
Collaring all that rebel blood

And the mercy seat is waiting
And I think my head is burning
And in a way I'm yearning
To be done with all this measuring of truth
An eye for an eye
And a tooth for a tooth
And anyway I told the truth
And I'm not afraid to die

And the mercy seat is burning
And I think my head is glowing
And in a way I'm hoping
To be done with all this weighing up of truth
An eye for an eye
And a tooth for a tooth
And I've got nothing left to lose
And I'm not afraid to die

And the mercy seat is glowing
And I think my head is smoking
And in a way I'm hoping
To be done with all these looks of disbelief
An eye for an eye
And a tooth for a tooth
And anyway there was no proof
Nor a motive why

And the mercy seat is smoking
And I think my head is melting
And in a way I'm helping
To be done with all this twisting of the truth
A lie for a lie
And a truth for a truth
And I've got nothing left to lose
And I'm not afraid to die

And the mercy seat is melting
And I think my blood is boiling
And in a way I'm spoiling
All the fun with all this truth and consequence
An eye for an eye
And a truth for a truth
And anyway I told the truth
And I'm not afraid to die

And the mercy seat is waiting
And I think my head is burning
And in a way I'm yearning
To be done with all this measuring of proof
A life for a life
And a truth for a truth
And anyway there was no proof
But I'm not afraid to tell a lie

And the mercy seat is waiting
And I think my head is burning
And in a way I'm yearning
To be done with all this measuring of truth
An eye for an eye
And a truth for a truth
And anyway I told the truth
But I'm afraid I told a lie

Up Jumped the Devil

O my, O my
What a wretched life
I was born on the day
That my poor mother died
I was cut from her belly
With a Stanley knife
My Daddy did a jig
With the drunk midwife

Who's that yonder all in flames
Dragging behind him a sack of chains
Who's that yonder all in flames
Up jumped the Devil and he staked his claim

O poor heart
I was doomed from the start
Doomed to play
The villain's part
I was the baddest Johnny
In the apple cart
My blood was blacker
Than the chambers of a dead nun's heart

Who's that milling on the courthouse steps
Nailing my face to the hitching fence
Who's that milling on the courthouse steps
Up jumped the Devil and off he crept

O no, O no
Where could I go
With my hump of trouble
And my sack of woe
To the digs and deserts of Mexico
Where my neck was safe from the lynching rope

Who's that yonder laughing at me
Like I was the brunt of some hilarity
Who's that yonder laughing at me
Up jumped the Devil 1, 2, 3

Ha ha ha
How lucky we were
We hit the cathouse
And sampled their wares
We got as drunk
As a couple of Czars
One night I spat out
My lucky star

Who's that dancing on the jailhouse roof
Stamping on the ramping with a cloven hoof
Who's that dancing on the jailhouse roof
Up jumped the Devil and said, 'Here is your man and I got proof'

O no, don't go, O no
O slow down, Joe
The righteous path
Is straight as an arrow
Take a walk
And you'll find it too narrow
Too narrow for the likes of me

Who's that hanging from the gallow tree
His eyes are hollow but he looks like me
Who's that hanging from the gallow tree
Up jumped the Devil and took my soul from me

Down we go, down we go
The Devil and me
Down we go, down we go
To Eternity
Down we go, down we go
We go down down down down down

Deanna

O DEANNA
O Deanna!
O DEANNA
Sweet Deanna!
O DEANNA
You know you are my friend, yeah
O DEANNA
And I ain't down here for your money
I ain't down here for your love
I ain't down here for your love or money
I'm down here for your soul

No carpet on the floor
And the winding-cloth holds many moths
Around your Ku Klux furniture
I cum a death's-head in your frock
We discuss the murder pact
We discuss the murder and the murder act
Murder takes the wheel of the Cadillac
And death climbs in the back

O DEANNA
This is a car
O DEANNA
This is a gun
O DEANNA
And this is day number one
O DEANNA
Our little crime-worn histories
Black and smoking Christmas trees

And honey, it ain't a mystery
Why you're a mystery to me

We will eat out of their pantries
And their parlours
Ashy leavings in their beds
And we'll unload into their heads
In this mean season
This little angel that I squeezin'
She ain't been mean to me

O DEANNA
O Deanna!
O DEANNA
You are my friend and my partner
O DEANNA
On this house on the hill
O DEANNA
And I ain't down here for your money
I ain't down here for your love
I ain't down here for your love or money
I'm down here for your soul

O DEANNA
I am a-knocking
O DEANNA
With my toolbox and my stocking
O DEANNA
And I'll meet you on the corner
O DEANNA
Yes, you point it like a finger
O DEANNA
And squeeze its little thing

O DEANNA
Feel its kick, hear its bang
And let's not worry about its issue
Don't worry about where it's been
And don't worry about where it hits
'Cause it just ain't yours to sin

O DEANNA
No, it just ain't yours to sin
O DEANNA
Sweet Deanna
O DEANNA
And we ain't getting any younger
O DEANNA
And I don't intend gettin' any older
O DEANNA
The sun a hump at my shoulder
O DEANNA
O Deanna!
O DEANNA
Sweet Deanna
O DEANNA
And I ain't down here for your money
I ain't down here for your love
I ain't down here for your love or money
I'm down here for your soul

Watching Alice

Alice wakes
It is morning
She is yawning
As she walks about the room
Her hair falls down her breast
She is naked and it is June
Standing at the window
I wonder if she knows that I can see
Watching Alice rise year after year
Up in her palace, she's captive there

Alice's body
Is golden brown
Her hair hangs down
As she brushes it one hundred times
First she pulls her stockings on
And then the church bell chimes
Alice climbs into her uniform
The zipper's on the side
Watching Alice dressing in her room
It's so depressing, it's cruel

Watching Alice dressing in her room
It's so depressing, it's true

Mercy

I stood in the water
In the middle month of winter
My camel skin was torture
I was in a state of nature
The wind, sir, it was wicked
I was so alone
Just as I predicted
My followers were gone

And I cried, 'Mercy
Have mercy on me'
And I got down on my knees

Thrown into a dungeon
Bread and water was my portion
Faith – my only weapon
To rest the Devil's legion
The speak-hole would slide open
A viper's voice would plead
Thick with innuendo
Syphilis and greed

And she cried, 'Mercy
Have mercy on me'
And I told her to get down on her knees

In a garden full of roses
My hands were tied behind me
My cousin was working miracles
I wondered if he'd find me
The moon was turned towards me

Like a platter made of gold
My death, it almost bored me
So often was it told

And I cried, 'Mercy'
I cried, 'Mercy on me'
Crying, 'Mercy
Have mercy on me'

City of Refuge

You better run
You better run and run and run
You better run, you better run
You better run to the City of Refuge
You better run, you better run
You better run to the City of Refuge

You stand before your maker
In a state of shame
Because your robes are covered in mud
While you kneel at the feet
Of a woman of the street
The gutters will run with blood
They will run with blood!

You better run, you better run
You better run to the City of Refuge
You better run, you better run
You better run to the City of Refuge

In the days of madness
My brother, my sister
When you're dragged toward the Hell-mouth
You will beg for the end
But there ain't gonna be one, friend
For the grave will spew you out
It will spew you out!

You better run, you better run
You better run to the City of Refuge
You better run, you better run
You better run to the City of Refuge

You'll be working in the darkness
Against your fellow man
And you'll find you're called to come forth
So you'll scrub and you'll scrub
But the trouble is, bub
The blood won't wash off
No, it won't come off!

You better run, you better run
You better run to the City of Refuge

You better run, you better run
You better run and run and run
You better run to the City of Refuge

Slowly Goes the Night

Lover, lover, goodbye
So slowly goes the night
I trace the print of your body with my hand
Like the map of some forbidden land
I trace the ghosts of your bones
With my trembling hand
Dark is my night
But darker is my day, yeah
I must've been blind
Out of my mind
Not to read the warning signs
How goes it?
It goes lonely
Goes slowly

So slowly goes the night
Ten lonely days, ten lonely nights
I watch the moon get flayed anew
Until the moon becomes the skinning tool
I send the skins of my sins out to cover and comfort you
I know of a Heaven
And honey I know of a Hell
I hang my head
In my bed
And remember what you said
'One evening, I'm leaving'
And I laughed and checked her breathing

Go slowly through the night
O baby, I feel the heel of time
I wake to find you sitting there
Cutting tangles out of your hair

Singing a song that's all wrong
Hey, but that's all right, I don't care
O darling, forgive me
For all the misery
I embrace an empty space
And your laughing song it fades
Where goes it?
It goes some place
Where it's lonely

And black as the night
Come back, darling and put things right
I hang my head and cry cry cry
Darling, all night I try
To seize on a reason for this mad mad season
The nights, they are so long now
I can't remember it being light
Call it sleep, call it death, call it what you like
But only sleep, dear
Only sleep brings you back to life
I hang my head
I toss and I sweat
I never never can forget
How goes it?
I'm going, but slowly slowly going
And we both know that it's gonna be all right

But it ain't you who has to cry cry cry
Ten lonely days, ten lonely nights
Since you left my side

Sunday's Slave

Sunday's got a slave
Monday's got one too
Sunday's got a slave
Monday's got one too
Our sufferings are countless
Our pleasures are a motley few
Spend all day digging my grave
Now go get Sunday's slave

Tuesday sleeps in the stable
Wednesday's in chains
Tuesday gathers up the crumbs under the table
Wednesday dare not complain
My heart has collapsed on the tracks of a run-away train
Just whisper his name
And here comes Sunday's slave

The hands in the stable are willing and able to pay
If you feel at a loss, man, as to who is the boss-man
Ask the blood on one of its bad days
For his nerve is to serve but the service is a mockery
He insists that he piss in your fist
But he still takes the money anyway
The master's a bastard
But don't tell Sunday's slave

Thursday's angered the master
OK, so Friday's gonna pay
Thursday's angered the master
Yeah, so Friday's gonna pay
One night on the rack and he's back saddling up Saturday

You can only whisper his name
But not on Sundays
Never on Sundays
O not on Sunday's slave

Sugar Sugar Sugar

Sugar sugar sugar
That man is bad
The road he drives you down
O sugar, it's a drag

That road it twists
That road is crossed
It's down that road
A lot of little girls go lost

Sugar sugar sugar
Keep on driving on
Until the City of Right
Becomes the City of Wrong

That stretch is long
You'll slip and slide
That stretch will find you
Gagged and tied

The hunter lies
In a lowly ditch
His eyes they sting
And his fingers twitch

You'll be his queen for the night
But in the morning you'll wake
With the lords and high ladies
Of the bottom of the lake

Sugar sugar sugar
That man is wild
And sugar, you know
That you're merely a child

He will laugh
And hang your sheets to see
The tokens of your virginity

Sugar sugar sugar
Honey, you're so sweet
And beside you, baby
Nothing can compete

Sugar sugar sugar
Honey, you're so sweet
But beside you, baby
A bad man sleeps

You better pray baby
Pray baby, pray baby
You better pray
You better pray baby
Pray baby, pray baby
You better pray baby

Sugar sugar sugar
That man is bad
And that's the bottom, baby
Coming right up ahead

You can smell his fear
You can smell his love
As he wipes his mouth
On your altar cloth

Sugar sugar sugar
Try to understand
I'm an angel of God
I'm your guardian

He smells your innocence
And like a dog he comes
And like all the dogs he is
I shut him down

Sugar sugar sugar
I can't explain
Must I kill that cocksucker
Every day

You better pray, baby
Pray baby, pray baby
You better pray
You better pray, baby
Pray baby, pray baby
You better pray

New Morning

One morn I awakened
A new sun was shining
The sky was a Kingdom
All covered in blood
The moon and the stars
Were the troops that lay conquered
Like fruit left to wither
Poor spiritual food

And the spears of the bright sun
All brave with its conquest
Did hover unearthly
In banners of fire
I knelt in the garden
Awash with the dawning
And a voice came so brightly
I covered my eyes

Thank you for giving
This bright new morning
So steeped seemed the evening
In darkness and blood
There'll be no sadness
There'll be no sorrow
There'll be no road too narrow
There'll be a new day
And it's today
For us

Girl at the Bottom of My Glass

Well, I can't raise my glass
Without seeing her ass
Through its telescopic bottom
I can't raise my glass
Without seeing her ass
Through its telescopic bottom
If you wanna know what animal it is
Ask the girl at the bottom of my glass

Well, lover come a-knocking
With my toolbag and my stocking
[. . .]
Well, lover come a-knocking
With my toolbag and my stocking
[. . .]
If you wanna know what's shaking down the house
Ask the girl at the bottom of my glass

I can't spill my drink
Without the woman at the sink
Coming round in her rubber mittens
I can't slop my drink
Without that woman at the sink
Coming at me in her rubber mittens
If you're looking for the woman of the house
Ask the girl at the bottom of my glass

I can't raise my drink
Without stopping to think
That some bad baby's giving me trouble
I can't raise my drink
Without stopping to think

That some bad baby's giving me trouble
If you wanna see what's inside of Sally
You'll find that girl in a hole out in the alley

I can't raise my glass
Without seeing her ass
This booze is turning bitter
I can't raise my glass
Without seeing her ass
I'm gunna jump right up and hit her

Well, you wanna know a little about my past
Take a squitch at the bitch in my house

That's What Jazz is to Me

Jazz
Fire-eating drag queens dressed as society whores
Crazy two-timing bitches running round
Ghetto-blasting blasters, blasting magnificently
Blossoms falling from the cherry trees
That's what jazz is to me
High buildings with crippled backs circle around my dreams
I clutch at the greasy tails of my dreams
White blossom falling from the cherry trees
That's what jazz is to me
Ten bottles standing in a row, military style
With hats pulled low over their brows
A thousand wasted hours
Skeletons entwined fucking and braying in the fields
Blossoms falling from the cherry tree
That's what jazz is to me
History repeating itself like a vindaloo
All the great cars of the world in one massive collision
All the doctors swallowed up by one incompetence
All the great theorists and teachers eaten alive . . .
Religious ecstasy and a blossom falling from a cherry tree
That's what jazz is to me
Blind fish being used as musical scales
Sharks puffed for fish and whales
I long to be by the sea where a blossom falls from a cherry
    tree
That's what jazz is for me
Three form, four form, five form, six form
Seven form, eight form, nine form
A blossom falling from the cherry tree
That's what jazz is for me
As Einstein said about his theory

I love it, I love it, I love it, I love jazz
It's in your heart, it's in your soul, it's in your mind
The colour of death, sweet vanilla essence
Richard Harris and Donald Pleasance
And a cherry blossom falling from a cherry tree
That's what jazz is to me

The Good Son
(1990)

Foi Na Cruz

Foi na cruz, foi na cruz
Que um dia
Meus pecados castigados em Jesus
Foi na cruz
Que um dia
Foi na cruz

Love comes a-knocking
Comes a-knocking upon our door
But you, you and me, love
We don't live there anymore

Foi na cruz, foi na cruz
Que um dia
Meus pecados castigados em Jesus
Foi na cruz
Que um dia
Foi na cruz

A little sleep, a little slumber
A little folding of the hands to sleep
A little love, a little hate, babe
A little trickery and deceit

Foi na cruz, foi na cruz
Que um dia
Meus pecados castigados em Jesus
Foi na cruz
Que um dia
Foi na cruz

Dream on 'til you can dream no more
For all our grand plans, babe
Will be dreams for ever more

Foi na cruz, foi na cruz
Que um dia
Meus pecados castigados em Jesus
Foi na cruz
Que um dia
Foi na cruz

Foi na cruz, foi na cruz
Que um dia
Meus pecados castigados em Jesus
Foi na cruz
Que um dia
Foi na cruz

The Good Son

One more man gone
One more man gone
One more man is gone
The good son walks into the field
He is a tiller, he has a tiller's hands
But down in his heart now
He lays down queer plans
Against his brother and against his family
Yet he worships his brother
And he worships his mother
But it's his father, he says, is an unfair man
The good son
The good son
The good son

The good son has sat and often wept
Beneath a malign star by which he's kept
And the night-time in which he's wrapped
Speaks of good and speaks of evil
And he calls to his mother
And he calls to his father
But they are deaf in the shadows of his brother's truancy
The good son
The good son
The good son

And he curses his mother
And he curses his father
And he curses his virtue like an unclean thing
The good son
The good son
The good son

One more man gone
One more man gone
One more man
One more man gone
One more man gone
One more man
One more man gone
One more man gone
One more man

One more man gone
One more man gone
One more man
One more man gone
One more man gone
One more man
One more man gone
One more man gone
One more man

Sorrow's Child

Sorrow's child
Sits by the river
Sorrow's child
Hears not the water
Sorrow's child
Sits by the river
Sorrow's child
Hears not the water
And just when it seems as though
You've got strength enough to stand
Sorrow's child all weak and strange
Stands waiting at your hand
Sorrow's child
Steps in the water
Sorrow's child
You follow after
Sorrow's child
Wades in deeper
Sorrow's child
Invites you under
And just when you thought as though
All your tears were wept and done
Sorrow's child grieves not what has passed
But all the past still yet to come
Sorrow's child
Sits by the water
Sorrow's child
Your arms enfold her
Sorrow's child
You're loath to befriend her
Sorrow's child
But in sorrow surrender

And just when it seems as though
All your tears were at an end
Sorrow's child lifts up her hand
And she brings it down again

The Weeping Song

Go, son, go down to the water
And see the women weeping there
Then go up into the mountains
The men, they are weeping too

Father, why are all the women weeping?
They are weeping for their men
Then why are all the men there weeping?
They are weeping back at them

This is a weeping song
A song in which to weep
While all the men and women sleep
This is a weeping song
But I won't be weeping long

Father, why are all the children weeping?
They are merely crying, son
O are they merely crying, father?
Yes, true weeping is yet to come

This is a weeping song
A song in which to weep
While all the little children sleep
This is a weeping song
But I won't be weeping long

O father, tell me, are you weeping?
Your face seems wet to touch
O then I'm so sorry, father
I never thought I hurt you so much

This is a weeping song
A song in which to weep
While we rock ourselves to sleep
This is a weeping song
But I won't be weeping long
No, I won't be weeping long
No, I won't be weeping long
No, I won't be weeping long

The Ship Song

Come sail your ships around me
And burn your bridges down
We make a little history, baby
Every time you come around

Come loose your dogs upon me
And let your hair hang down
You are a little mystery to me
Every time you come around

We talk about it all night long
We define our moral ground
But when I crawl into your arms
Everything comes tumbling down

Come sail your ships around me
And burn your bridges down
We make a little history, baby
Every time you come around

Your face has fallen sad now
For you know the time is nigh
When I must remove your wings
And you, you must try to fly

Come sail your ships around me
And burn your bridges down
We make a little history, baby
Every time you come around

Come loose your dogs upon me
And let your hair hang down
You are a little mystery to me
Every time you call around

The Hammer Song

I set out on Monday
The night was cold and vast
And my brother slept
And though I left quite quietly
My father raged and raged
And my mother wept

Now my life was like a river
All sucked into the ground
And then the hammer came down
Lord, the hammer came down

Many miles did I roam
Through the ice and through the snow
My horse died on the seventh day

I stumbled into a city
Where the people tried to kill me
And I ran in shame
Then I came upon a river
And I laid my saddle down
And then the hammer came down
Lord, the hammer came down
It knocked me to the ground
And I said, 'Please, please
Take me back to my hometown'
Lord, the hammer came down

Now I've been made weak by visions
Many visions did I see
All through the night

On the seventh hour an angel came
With many snakes in all his hands
And I fled in fright

I pushed off into the river
And the water came around
And then the hammer came down
Lord, the hammer came down
And it did not make a sound
And I said, 'Please, please
Take me back to my home ground'
Lord, the hammer came down

Lament

I've seen your fairground hair
Your seaside eyes
Your vampire tooth, your little truth
Your tiny lies

I know your trembling hand, your guilty prize
Your sleeping limbs, your foreign hymns
Your midnight cries

So dry your eyes
And turn your head away
Now there's nothing more to say
Now you're gone away

I know your trail of tears, your slip of hand
Your monkey paw, your monkey claw
And your monkey hand

I've seen your trick of blood, your trap of fire
Your ancient wound, your scarlet moon
And your jailhouse smile

So dry your eyes
And turn your head away
Now there's nothing more to say
Now you're gone away

I'll miss your urchin smile, your orphan tears
Your shining prize, your tiny cries
Your little fears

I'll miss your fairground hair
Your seaside eyes
Your vampire tooth, your little truth
And your tiny lies

So dry your eyes
And turn your head away
Now there's nothing more to say
Now you're gone away

So dry your eyes
And turn your head away
Now there's nothing more to say
Now you're gone away

The Witness Song

Yeah, yeah
Well, well
I took a walk down to the port
Where strangers meet and do consort
All blinkered with desire
And a winter fog moved thickly on
A winter fog moved thickly on
A winter fog moved thickly on

Now who will be the witness
When the fog's too thick to see

And I saw a friend beside a wall
Her hands were raised in supplication
And her face I could not see at all
And I raised my hands in rage
And brought them down again
And we entered through the eastern door
And I entered through the eastern door
And she entered through the eastern door

Now who will be the witness
When you're all too blind to see
O yes, yes, yes

And time gets somewhat muddied here
But no matter, no matter
Here come the events all tumbling down
Now beyond the wall was a great garden
Into which we passed
Me and my friend
And the place was all overgrown with weeds

And behold from its centre there rose a great fountain
The fountain with the healing waters
And we knelt down by the rim

And I dipped my hand in
And she dipped her hand in too
And I said, 'Are you healed?'
And she said, 'Well, are you healed?'
And I said, 'Yes, I'm healed'
And she said, 'Well, yes, I'm healed then too'
And I said, 'Babe, you are a liar'
'Babe, you are a liar'
'Babe, you are a liar, too'
Now, who will be the witness
When you're all too healed to see

And I kissed her once, I kissed her twice
And made my way to leave her
And she raised her hand up to her face
And brought it down again
I said, 'That gesture, it will haunt me
That gesture, it will haunt me'
And I left there by the eastern door
She left there by the western door

Now who will be the witness
When you're blind and you can't see
Who will be the witness
When you're all so clean and you cannot see
Who will be the witness there
When your friends are everywhere
Who will be the witness there
And your enemies have ceased to care

Lucy

Last night I lay trembling
The moon it was low
It was the end of love
Of misery and woe

Then suddenly above me
Her face buried in light
Came a vision of beauty
All covered in white

Now the bell-tower is ringing
And the night has stole past
O Lucy, can you hear me?
Wherever you rest

I'll love her for ever
I'll love her for all time
I'll love her 'til the stars
Fall down from the sky

Now the bell-tower is ringing
And I shake on the floor
O Lucy, can you hear me?
When I call and call

Now the bell-tower is ringing
And the moon it is high
O Lucy, can you hear me?
When I cry and cry and cry

The Train Song

Tell me, how long the train's been gone?
Tell me, how long the train's been gone?
And was she there?
And was she there?
Tell me, how long the train's been gone?

Tell me, how many coaches long?
Tell me, how many coaches long?
What did she wear?
What did she wear?
Tell me, how many coaches long?

Tell me, when did the whistle blow?
Tell me, when did the whistle blow?
And did she dye her hair?
And did she dye her hair?
Tell me, when did the whistle blow?

Tell me, how long the train's been gone?
Tell me, how long the train's been gone?
And was she there?
And was she there?
Tell me, how long the train's been gone?

Henry’s Dream
(1992)

Papa Won't Leave You, Henry
I Had a Dream, Joe
Straight to You
Brother, My Cup is Empty
Christina the Astonishing
When I First Came to Town
John Finn's Wife
Loom of the Land
Jack the Ripper

Faraway, So Close!
Cassiel's Song
Blue Bird

Papa Won't Leave You, Henry

I went out walking the other day
The wind hung wet around my neck
My head it rang with screams and groans
From the night I spent amongst her bones
I passed beside the mission house
Where that mad old buzzard, the Reverend,
Shrieked and flapped about life after you're dead
Well, I thought about my friend, Michel
How they rolled him in linoleum
And shot him in the neck
A bloody halo like a think-bubble
Circling his head
And I bellowed at the firmament
Looks like the rains are here to stay
And the rain pissed down upon me
And washed me all away
Saying
Papa won't leave you, Henry
Papa won't leave you, Boy
Papa won't leave you, Henry
Papa won't leave you, Boy
Well, the road is long
And the road is hard
And many fall by the side
But Papa won't leave you, Henry
So there ain't no need to cry

And I went on down the road
He went on down the road
And I went on down the road
He went on down the road

Well, the moon it looked exhausted
Like something you should pity
Spent and age-spotted
Above the sizzling wires of the city
Well, it reminded me of her face
Her bleached and hungry eyes
Her hair was like a curtain
Falling open with the laughter
And closing with the lies
But the ghost of her still lingers on
Though she's passed through me and is gone
The slum dogs, they are barking
And the rain children on the streets
And the tears that we will weep today
Will all be washed way
By the tears that we will weep again tomorrow
Papa won't leave you, Henry
Papa won't leave you, Boy
Papa won't leave you, Henry
Papa won't leave you, Boy
For the road is long
And the road is hard
And many fall by the side
But Papa won't leave you, Henry
So there ain't no need to cry

And I went on down the road
He went on down the road
And I went on down the road
He went on down the road

And I came upon a little house
A little house upon a hill
And I entered through – the curtain hissed –
Into the house with its blood-red bowels
Where wet-lipped women with greasy fists
Crawled the ceilings and the walls
They filled me full of drink
And led me round the rooms
Naked and cold and grinning
Until everything went black
And I came down spinning
I awoke so drunk and full of rage
That I could hardly speak
A fag in a whale-bone corset
Draping his dick across my cheek
And it's into the shame
And it's into the guilt
And it's into the fucking fray
And the walls ran red around me
A warm arterial spray
Saying
Papa won't leave you, Henry
Papa won't leave you, Boy
Papa won't leave you, Henry
Papa won't leave you, Boy
Well, the night is dark
And the night is deep
And its jaws are open wide
But Papa won't leave you, Henry
So there ain't no need to cry

And I went on down the road
He went on down the road
And I went on down the road
He went on down the road

It's the rainy season where I'm living
Death comes leaping out of every doorway
Wasting you for your money, for your clothes
And for your nothing
Entire towns being washed away
Favelas exploding on inflammable spillways
Lynch-mobs, death squads, babies being born without brains
The mad heat and the relentless rains
And if you stick your arm into that hole
It comes out sheared off to the bone
And with her kisses bubbling on my lips
I swiped the rain and nearly missed
And I went on down the road
He went on down the road
Singing
Papa won't leave you, Henry
Papa won't leave you, Boy
Papa won't leave you, Henry
Papa won't leave you, Boy
Well, the road is long
And the road is hard
And many fall by the side
But Papa won't leave you, Henry
So there ain't no need to cry

And I went on down the road
He went on down the road
And I went on down the road
He went on down the road
Bent beneath my heavy load
Under his heavy load
Yeah, I went on down the road
Yeah, he went on down the road

Woah, woah
Woah, woah
Woah, woah
Woah, woah
And I went on down that road

I Had a Dream, Joe

I had a dream
I had a dream
I had a dream, Joe

I had a dream, Joe
You were standing in the middle of an open road
I had a dream, Joe
Your hands were raised up to the sky
And your mouth was covered in foam
I had a dream, Joe
A shadowy Jesus flitted from tree to tree
I had a dream, Joe
And a society of whores stuck needles in an image of me
I had a dream, Joe
It was Autumn time and thickly fell the leaves
And in that dream, Joe
A pimp in a seersucker suit sucked a toothpick
And pointed his finger at me

I had a dream
I had a dream
I had a dream, Joe

I opened my eyes, Joe
The night had been a giant, dribbling and pacing the boards
I opened my eyes, Joe
All your letters and cards stacked up against the door
I opened my eyes, Joe
The morning light came slowly tumbling through the crack
In the window, Joe
And I thought of you and I felt like I was lugging
A body on my back

I had a dream
I had a dream
I had a dream, Joe

Where did you go, Joe?
On that endless, senseless, demented drift
Where did you go, Joe?
Into the woods, into the trees, where you move and shift
Where did you go, Joe?
All dressed up in your ridiculous seersucker suit
Where did you go, Joe?
With that strew of wreckage
Forever at the heel of your boot

I had a dream
I had a dream
I had a dream, Joe
I had a dream
I had a dream
I had a dream, Joe

Straight to You

All the towers of ivory are crumbling
And the swallows have sharpened their beaks
This is the time of our great undoing
This is the time that I'll come running
Straight to you
For I am captured
Straight to you
For I am captured
One more time

The light in our window is fading
The candle gutters on the ledge
Well, now, sorrow, it comes a-stealing
And I'll cry, girl, but I'll come a-running
Straight to you
For I am captured
Straight to you
For I am captured
One more time

Gone are the days of rainbows
Gone are the nights of swinging from the stars
For the sea will swallow up the mountains
And the sky will throw thunder-bolts and sparks
Straight at you
But I'll come a-running
Straight to you
But I'll come a-running
One more time

Heaven has denied us its kingdom
The saints are drunk and howling at the moon
The chariots of angels are colliding
Well, I'll run, babe, but I'll come running
Straight to you
For I am captured
Straight to you
For I am captured
One more time

Brother, My Cup is Empty

Brother, my cup is empty
And I haven't got a penny
For to buy no more whiskey
I have to go home

I am the captain of my pain
'Tis the bit, the bridle
The thrashing cane
The stirrup, the harness
The whipping mane
The pickled eye
The shrinking brain
O brother, buy me one more drink
I'll explain the nature of my pain
Yes, let me tell you once again
I am the captain of my pain

O brother, my cup is empty
And I haven't got a penny
For to buy no more whiskey
I have to go home

I cannot blame it all on her
To blame her all would be a lie
For many a night I lay awake
And wished that I could watch her die
To see her accusing finger spurt
To see flies swarm her hateful eye
To watch her groaning in the dirt
To see her clicking tongue crack dry

O brother, buy me one more drink
One more drink and then goodbye
And do not mock me when I say
Let's drink one more before I die

O brother, my cup is empty
And I haven't got a penny
For to buy no more whiskey
I have to go home

Well, I've been sliding down on rainbows
I've been swinging from the stars
Now this wretch in beggar's clothing
Bangs his cup across the bars
Look, this cup of mine is empty!
Seems I've misplaced my desires
Seems I'm sweeping up the ashes
Of all my former fires
So brother, be a brother
And fill this tiny cup of mine
And please, sir, make it whiskey
For I have no head for wine

O brother, my cup is empty
And I haven't got a penny
For to buy no more whiskey
I have to go home

I counted up my blessings
And I counted only one
One tiny little blessing
And now that blessing's gone
So buy me one more drink, my brother

Then I'm taking to the road
Yes, I'm taking to the rain
I'm taking to the snow
O my friend, my only brother
Do not let the party grieve
So throw a dollar on to the bar
Now kiss my ass and leave

O brother, my cup is empty
And I haven't got a penny
For to buy no more whiskey
I have to go home

Christina the Astonishing

Christina the Astonishing
Lived a long long time ago
She was stricken with a seizure
At the age of twenty-two
They took her body in a coffin
To a tiny church in Liège
Where she sprang up from the coffin
Just after the Agnus Dei
She soared up to the rafters
Perched on a beam up there
Cried, 'The stink of human sin
Is more than I can bear'
Christina the Astonishing
Was the most astonishing of all
She prayed balanced on a hurdle
Or curled up into a ball
She fled to remote places
Climbed towers and trees and walls
To escape the stench of human corruption
Into an oven she did crawl
O Christina the Astonishing
Behaved in a terrifying way
She would run wildly through the streets
Jump in the Meuse and swim away
O Christina the Astonishing
Behaved in a terrifying way
Died at the age of seventy-four
In the convent of St Anna

When I First Came to Town

When I first came to town
All the people gathered round
They bought me drinks
Lord, how quickly they changed their tune

When I first came to town
People took me round from end to end
Like someone may take round a friend
O how quickly they changed their tune

Suspicion and dark murmurs surround me
Everywhere I go they confound me
As though the blood on my hands
Is there for every citizen to see

O sweet Jesus
There is no turning back
There is always one more town
A little further down the track

And from my window, across the tracks
I watch the juicers burn their fires
And in that light
Their faces leer at me
How I wish they'd just let me be

When I first came to town
Their favours were for free
Now even the doors of the whores of this town
Are closed to me

I search the mirror
And I try to see
Why the people of this town
Have washed their hands of me

O sweet Jesus
There is no turning back
There is always one more town
A little further down the track

O Lord, every God-damn turn I take
I fear the noose, I fear the stake
For there is no bone
They did not break
In all the towns I've been before

Well, those that sin against me are snuffed out
I know that from every day that I live
God-damn the day that I was born
The night that forced me from the womb
And God-damn this town
For I am leaving now
But one day I will return
And the people of this town will surely see
Just how quickly the tables turn

O sweet Jesus
This really is the end
There is always one more town
A little further round the bend

John Finn's Wife

Well, the night was deep and the night was dark
And I was at the old dance-hall on the edge of town
Some big ceremony was going down
Dancers writhed and squirmed and then
Came apart and then writhed again
Like squirming flies on a pin
In the heat and in the din
Yes, in the heat and in the din
I fell to thinking about the brand new wife of mad John
Finn

Well, midnight came and a clock did strike
And in she came, did John Finn's wife
With legs like scissors and butcher's knives
A tattooed breast and flaming eyes
And a crimson carnation in her teeth
Carving her way through the dance floor
And I'm standing over by the bandstand
Every eye gaping on John Finn's wife
Yeah, every eye gaping on John Finn's wife

Now John Finn's wife was something of a mystery
In a town where to share a sworn secret was a solemn duty
I had brass knuckles and a bolo knife
Over near the bandstand with John Finn's wife
She got perfumed breasts and raven hair
Sprinkled with wedding confettis
And a gang of garrotters were all giving me stares
Armed, as they were, with machetes
And the night through the window was full of lights
Winking and a-watching at John Finn's wife

Next came the cops, all out on the town
But it don't look like no trouble there
As they head for the bar in their lumpy suits
And I slip my hand between the legs of John Finn's wife
And they seemed to yawn awake, her thighs
It was a warm and very ferocious night
The moon was full of blood and light
And my eyes grew small and my eyes grew tight
As I plotted in the ear of John Finn's wife

Enter John Finn in his shrunken suit
With his quick black eyes and black cheroot
With his filed-down teeth and a hobnail boot
And his fists full of pistols in his pockets
Aiming at me and aiming at his wife
The band fall silent fearing for their lives
And with fear in my guts like tangled twine
'Cause all I got is brass knuckles and a bolo knife
And mad John Finn's wife is all
And the three of us walk out of the hall

Now the night bore down upon us all
You could hear the crickets in the thickets call
And guns did flare and guns did bawl
And I planted my bolo knife in the neck
Of mad John Finn. I took his wretched life
Now I'm over by the bandstand
Every hand moving on John Finn's wife
Every hand moving on John Finn's wife

And John Finn's wife
Took all the flowers down from her hair
And threw them on the ground
And the flies did hum

And the flies did buzz around
Poor John Finn
Lying dead upon the ground
Lying dead upon the ground

Loom of the Land

It was the dirty end of winter
Along the loom of the land
When I walked with sweet Sally
Hand upon hand

And the wind it bit bitter
For a boy of no means
With no shoes on his feet
And a knife in his jeans

Along the loom of the land
The mission bells peeled
From the tower at Saint Mary's
Down to Reprobate Fields

And I saw that the world
Was all blessed and bright
And Sally breathed softly
In the majestic night

O baby, please don't cry
And try to keep
Your little head upon my shoulder
Now go to sleep

The elms and the poplars
Were turning their backs
Past the rumbling station
We followed the tracks

We found an untrodden path
And followed it down
The moon in the sky
Like a dislodged crown

My hands they burned
In the folds of her coat
Breathing milky white air
From deep in her throat

O baby, please don't cry
And try to keep
Your little head upon my shoulder
Now go to sleep

I told Sally in whispers
I'll never bring you harm
Her breast it was small
And warm in my palm

I told her the moon
Was a magical thing
That it shone gold in the winter
And silver in spring

And we walked and walked
Across the endless sands
Just me and my Sally
Along the loom of the land

O baby, please don't cry
And try to keep
Your little head upon my shoulder
Now go to sleep

Jack the Ripper

I got a woman
She rules my house with an iron fist
I got a woman
She rules my house with an iron fist
She screams out Jack the Ripper
Every time I try to give that girl a kiss

I got a woman
She strikes me down with a fist of lead
I got a woman
She strikes me down with a fist of lead
We bed in a bucket of butcher's knives
I awake with a hatchet hanging over my head

Well, you know the story of the viper
It's long and lean with a poison tooth
Yeah, you know the story of the viper
It's long and lean with a poison tooth
Well, they're hissing under the floorboards
Hanging down in bunches from my roof

I got a woman
She just hollers what she wants from where she is
I got a woman
She just hollers what she wants from where she is
She screams out Jack the Ripper
Every time I try to give that girl a kiss

Faraway, So Close!

Empty out your pockets, toss the lot upon the floor
All those treasures, my friend, you don't need them anymore
Your days are all through dying, they gave all their ghosts
away
So kiss close all of your wounds and call living life a day

The planets gravitate around you
And the stars shower down around you
And the angels in Heaven adore you
And the saints they all stand and applaud you
So faraway, so faraway and yet so close

Say farewell to the passing of the years
Though all your sweet goodbyes will fall upon deaf ears
Kiss softly the mouths of the ones you love
Beneath the September moon and the heavens above

And the world will turn without you
And history will soon forget about you
But the heavens they will reward you
And the saints will all be there to escort you
So faraway, so faraway and yet so close

Do not grieve at the passing of mortality
For life's but a thing of terrible gravity
And the planets gravitate around you
And the stars shower down about you
And the angels in Heaven adore you
While those saints they all stand and applaud you
So faraway, so faraway and yet so close

Cassiel's Song

We've come to bring you home
Haven't we, Cassiel?

To cast aside your loss and all of your sadness
And shuffle off that mortal coil and mortal madness
For we're here to pick you up and bring you home
Aren't we, Cassiel?

It's a place where you did not belong
Where time itself was mad and far too strong
Where life leapt up laughing and hit you head on and hurt
  you
Didn't it hurt you, Cassiel?

While time outran you and trouble flew toward you
And you were there to greet it
Weren't you, foolish Cassiel?

But here we are, we've come to call you home
And here you'll stay, never more to stray
Where you can kick off your boots of clay
Can't you, Cassiel?

For death and you did recklessly collide
And time ran out of you, and you ran out of time
Didn't you, Cassiel?

And all the clocks in all the world
May this once just skip a beat in memory of you
But then again those damn clocks, they probably won't
Will they, Cassiel?

One moment you are there
Then strangely you are gone
But on behalf of us all here
We're glad to have you home
Aren't we, dear Cassiel?

Blue Bird

I got a blue bird
A blue bird on my shoulder
I got a blue bird
A blue bird on my shoulder

I saw her standing
Standing by the water
She was naked
Her hair in great disorder

And I know why I'm flying
And the rest is lies

I sent a warning
A warning of disaster
I sent a warning
I warned of great disaster

I sent that blue bird
That blue bird down the water
I sent that blue bird
Floating down the water

And I know that I'm flying
And the rest is lies

And I know that I'm flying
And the rest is lies

Let Love In
(1994)

Do You Love Me?
Nobody's Baby Now
Loverman
Jangling Jack
Red Right Hand
I Let Love In
Thirsty Dog
Ain't Gonna Rain Anymore
Lay Me Low
Do You Love Me? (Part 2)

Sail Away
(I'll Love You) Till the End of the World
What Can I Give You?

Do You Love Me?

I found her on a night of fire and noise
Wild bells rang in a wild sky
I knew from that moment on
I'd love her 'til the day that I died
And I kissed away a thousand tears
My Lady of the Various Sorrows
Some begged, some borrowed, some stolen
Some kept safe for tomorrow
On an endless night, silver star-spangled
The bells from the chapel went jingle-jangle

Do you love me?
Do you love me?
Do you love me
Like I love you?

She was given to me to put things right
And I stacked all my accomplishments beside her
Still I seemed obsolete and small
I found God and all His Devils inside her
In my bed she cast the blizzard out
A mock sun blazed upon her head
So completely filled with light she was
Her shadow fanged and hairy and mad
Our love-lines grew hopelessly tangled
And the bells from the chapel went jingle-jangle

Do you love me?
Do you love me?
Do you love me
Like I love you?

She had a heartful of love and devotion
She had a mindful of tyranny and terror
Well, I try, I do, I really try
But I just err, baby, I do, I error

So come find me, my darling one
I'm down to the grounds, the very dregs
Ah, here she comes, blocking the sun
Blood running down the inside of her legs
The moon in the sky is battered and mangled
And the bells from the chapel go jingle-jangle

Do you love me?
Do you love me?
Do you love me
Like I love you?

All things move toward their end
I knew before I met her that I would lose her
I swear I made every effort to be good to her
I swear I made every effort not to abuse her
Crazy bracelets on her wrists and her ankles
And the bells from the chapel went jingle-jangle

Do you love me?
Do you love me?
Do you love me
Like I love you?

Nobody's Baby Now

I've searched the holy books
Tried to unravel the mystery of Jesus Christ the Saviour
I've read the poets and the analysts
Searched through the books on human behaviour
I travelled the whole world around
For an answer that refused to be found
I don't know why and I don't know how
But she's nobody's baby now

I loved her then and I guess I love her still
Hers is the face I see when a certain mood moves in
She lives in my blood and skin
Her wild feral stare, her dark hair
Her winter lips as cold as stone
Yeah, I was her man
But there are some things even love won't allow
I held her hand but I don't hold it now
I don't know why and I don't know how
But she's nobody's baby now

This is her dress that I loved best
With the blue quilted violets across the breast
And these are my many letters
Torn to pieces by her long-fingered hand
I was her cruel-hearted man
And though I've tried to lay her ghost down
She's moving through me, even now
I don't know why and I don't know how
But she's nobody's baby now

Loverman

There's a devil waiting outside your door
(How much longer)
Bucking and braying and pawing at the floor
Well, he's howling with pain and crawling up the walls
There's a Devil waiting outside your door
He's weak with evil and broken by the world
He's shouting your name and asking for more
There's a devil waiting outside your door

Loverman! Since the world began
For ever, Amen 'til the end of time
Take off that dress, I'm coming down
I'm your Loverman!
'Cause I am what I am what I am what I am

L is for LOVE baby
O is for ONLY you that I do
V is for loving VIRTUALLY everything that you are
E is for loving almost EVERYTHING that you do
R is for RAPE me
M is for MURDER me
A is for ANSWERING all of my prayers
N is for KNOWING your Loverman's going to be
  the answer to all of yours

I'll be your Loverman 'til the bitter end
While empires burn down
For ever and ever and ever and ever, Amen
I'm your Loverman!
So help me, baby, so help me
'Cause I am what I am what I am what I am
I'm your Loverman!

There's a devil crawling along your floor
With a trembling heart, he's coming through your door
With his straining sex in his jumping paw
There's a devil crawling along your floor
And he's old and he's stupid and he's hungry and he's
sore
And he's blind and he's lame and he's dirty and he's
poor
There's a devil crawling along your floor

Loverman! Here I stand for ever, Amen
'Cause I am what I am what I am what I am
Forgive me, baby, my hands are tied
And I got no choice, no, I got no choice at all

I'll say it again

L is for LOVE, baby
O is for O yes I do
V is for VIRTUE, so I ain't gonna hurt you
E is for EVEN if you want me to
R is for RENDER unto me, baby
M is for that which is MINE
A is for ANY old how, darling
N is for ANY old time

I'll be your Loverman! I got a masterplan
To take off your dress and be your man
Seize the throne, seize the mantle
Seize the crown
'Cause I am what I am what I am what I am
I'm your Loverman!

There's a devil lying by your side
You might think he's asleep but take a look at his eyes
He wants you, darling, to be his bride
There's a devil lying by your side

Loverman! Loverman!

Jangling Jack

Jangling Jack
Goes, 'Yackety yack'
Visits the home of the brave
Hails a fat yellow cab
Jack wanna celebrate
Jack wanna big drink
Driver drops him at a bar
Called the Rinky Dink
Jack pushes through the door
And crosses the floor
Tips his hat to a man
Grinning in the corner
Going, 'Do da do do da do'

Says, 'I'm Jangling Jack
I go, "Do da do"
I wanna Rinky Dink Special
I wanna little umbrella too'
Jack flops on his stool
Sees the grinning man laugh
So Jack laughs back
Jack raises his glass
Says, 'God bless this country
And everything in it
The losers and the winners
The good guys and the sinners'
The grinning man says, 'Buddy
It's all yackety yack'
Whips out a little black pistol
Shoots a bullet in Jack

Jangling Jack
Do da do do da do
Jangling Jack
How do you do da do

Jangling Jack flies off his seat
Crashes through the door
Lands in a heap on the street
Hears his mother's voice
Going, 'Do da do'
Jack is shouting
'Mummy, is that you?'
He sees the berserk city
Sees the dead stacked in piles
Sees the screaming crowd
Screams, 'Where in Hell am I?'
Going, 'Do da do'
Going, 'Do da do'

Well, Jangling Jack
As a matter of fact
Crawls through the crowd
Back into the bar
Jack crawls to his stool
Jack drags himself up
Falls back down on his arse
In a puddle of blood
Going, 'Goodbye, Mummy
Goodbye, goodbye'
Jack doubles over
And he vomits and dies
Going, 'Do da do'
Going, 'Do da do'

Red Right Hand

Take a little walk to the edge of town
Go across the tracks
Where thc viaduct looms like a bird of doom
As it shifts and cracks
Where secrets lie in the border fires, in the humming
  wires
Hey man, you know you're never coming back
Past the square, past the bridge, past the mills, past the
  stacks
On a gathering storm comes a tall handsome man
In a dusty black coat with a red right hand

He'll wrap you in his arms, tell you that you've been a good
  boy
He'll rekindle all those dreams it took you a lifetime to
  destroy
He'll reach deep into the hole, heal your shrinking soul
Hey buddy, you know you're never ever coming back
He's a ghost, he's a god, he's a man, he's a guru
They're whispering his name across this disappearing
  land
But hidden in his coat is a red right hand

You ain't got no money? He'll get you some
You ain't got no car? He'll get you one
You ain't got no self-respect, you feel like an insect
Well, don't you worry, buddy, 'cause here he comes
Through the ghetto and the barrio and the bowery and the
  slum
A shadow is cast wherever he stands
Stacks of green paper in his red right hand

You'll see him in your nightmares, you'll see him in your dreams
He'll appear out of nowhere but he ain't what he seems
You'll see him in your head, on the TV screen
And hey buddy, I'm warning you to turn it off
He's a ghost, he's a god, he's a man, he's a guru
You're one microscopic cog in his catastrophic plan
Designed and directed by his red right hand

I Let Love In

Despair and Deception, Love's ugly little twins
Came a-knocking on my door, I let them in
Darling, you're the punishment for all my former sins

I let love in

The door it opened just a crack, but Love was shrewd and bold
My life flashed before my eyes, it was a horror to behold
A life-sentence sweeping confetti from the floor of a concrete hole

I let love in

Well, I've been bound and gagged and I've been terrorized
And I've been castrated and I've been lobotomized
But never has my tormenter come in such a cunning disguise

I let love in

O Lord, tell me what I done
Please don't leave me here on my own
Where are my friends?
My friends are gone

So if you're sitting all alone and hear a knocking at your door
And the air is full of promises, well buddy, you've been warned
Far worse to be Love's lover than the lover that Love has scorned

I let love in

Thirsty Dog

I know you've heard it all before
But I'm sorry for this three-year war
For the setting up of camps and wire and trenches
I'm sorry for the other night
I know sorry don't make it right
I'm sorry for things I can't even mention

I'm sorry sorry sorry, sorry
I'm sitting feeling sorry in the Thirsty Dog
I'm sorry sorry sorry, sorry
I'm feeling very sorry in the Thirsty Dog

You keep nailing me back into my box
I'm sorry I keep popping back up
With my crazy mouth and jangling jester's cap
I'm sorry I ever wrote that book
I'm sorry about the way I look
But there ain't a lot that I can do about that

I'm sorry sorry sorry, sorry
I'm sitting feeling sorry in the Thirsty Dog
I'm sorry sorry sorry, sorry
I'm feeling very sorry in the Thirsty Dog

I'm sorry about the hospital
Some things are unforgivable
Some things simply cannot be forgiven
I was not equipped to know how to care
And on the occasions I came up for air
I saw my life and wondered what the hell had I been living

I'm sorry sorry sorry, sorry
I'm sitting feeling sorry in the Thirsty Dog
I'm sorry sorry sorry, sorry
I'm feeling very sorry in the Thirsty Dog

I'm sorry about all your friends
I hope they'll speak to me again
I said before I'd pay for all the damage
I'm sorry it's just rotten luck
I'm sorry I've forgotten how to fuck
It's just that I think my heart and soul are kind of famished

I'm sorry sorry sorry, sorry
I'm sitting feeling sorry in the Thirsty Dog
I'm sorry sorry sorry, sorry
I'm feeling very sorry in the Thirsty Dog

Forgive me, darling, but don't worry
Love is always having to say you're sorry
And I am, from my head down to my shoes
I'm sorry that I'm always pissed
I'm sorry that I exist
And when I look into your eyes
I can see you're sorry too

I'm sorry sorry sorry, sorry
I'm sitting feeling sorry in the Thirsty Dog
I'm sorry sorry sorry, sorry
I'm feeling very sorry in the Thirsty Dog

Ain't Gonna Rain Anymore

Once there came a storm in the form of a girl
It blew to pieces my snug little world
And sometimes I swear I can still hear her howl
Down through the wreckage and the ruins

And it ain't gonna rain anymore
Now my baby's gone
And it ain't gonna rain anymore
Now my baby's gone

Now the storm has passed over me
I'm left to drift on a dead calm sea
And watch her for ever through the cracks in the beams
Nailed across the doorways of the bedrooms of my dreams

And it ain't gonna rain anymore
Now my baby's gone
And it ain't gonna rain anymore
Now my baby's gone

Now I have no one to hold
Now I am all alone again
It ain't too hot and it ain't too cold
And there is no sign of rain

And it ain't gonna rain anymore
Now my baby's gone, yeah
And it ain't gonna rain anymore
Now my baby's gone, yeah
And I'm on my own

She ain't coming back no more
She ain't coming back no more
She ain't coming back no more
Say what you will, I don't care

Lay Me Low

They're gonna lay me low
They're gonna sink me in the snow
They're gonna throw back their heads and crow
When I go

They're gonna jump and shout
They're gonna wave their arms about
All the stories will come out
When I go

All the stars will glow bright
My friends will give up the fight
They'll see my work in a different light
When I go

They'll try telephoning my mother
They'll end up getting my brother
Who'll spill the story on some long-gone lover
I hardly know

Hats off to the man
On top of the world
Come crawl up here, baby
And I'll show you how it works
If you wanna be my friend
And you wanna repent
And you want it all to end
And you wanna know when
Then take a bow
Do it now, do it any old how
Make a stand, take my hand
And blow it all to Hell

They'll inform the police chief
Who will breathe a sigh of relief
He'll say I was a malanderer, a badlander and a thief
When I go

They will interview my teachers
Who'll say I was one of God's sorrier creatures
There'll be informative six-page features
When I go

They'll bang a big old gong
The motorcade will be ten miles long
The world will join together for a farewell song
When they put me down below

They'll sound a flugelhorn
The sea will rage, the sky will storm
All man and beast will mourn
When I go

Hats off to the man
On top of the world
Crawl over here, darling
And we can watch this damn thing turn
If you wanna be my friend
And you wanna repent
And you want it all to end
And you wanna know when
Then do it now
Don't care how, do it any old how
Take my hand, make a stand
And blow it all to Hell

Do You Love Me? (Part 2)

Onward! And onward! And onward I go!
Where no man before could be bothered to go
'Til the soles of my shoes are shot full of holes
And it's all downhill with a bullet
This ramblin' and rovin' has taken its course
I'm grazing with the dinosaurs and the dear old horses
And the city streets crack and a great hole forces
Me down with my soapbox, my pulpit
The theatre ceiling is silver star-spangled
And the coins in my pocket go jingle-jangle

Do you love me?
Do you love me?
Do you love me?
Do you love me?

There's a man in the theatre with girlish eyes
Who's holding my childhood to ransom
On the screen there's a death, there's a rustle of cloth
And a sickly voice calling me handsome
There's a man in the theatre with sly girlish eyes
On the screen there's an ape, a gorilla
There's a groan, there's a cough, there's a rustle of cloth
And a voice that stinks of death and vanilla
This is a secret, mauled and mangled
And the coins in my pocket go jingle-jangle

Do you love me?
Do you love me?
Do you love me?
Do you love me?

The walls of the ceiling are painted in blood
The lights go down, the red curtains come apart
The room is full of smoke and dialogue I know by heart
And the coins in my pocket go jingle-jangle
As the great screen crackled and popped
The clock of my boyhood was wound down and stopped
And my handsome little body oddly propped
And my trousers right down to my ankles
Yes, it's onward! And upward!
And I'm off to find love
Do you love me? If you do, I'm thankful

Do you love me?
Do you love me?
Do you love me?
Do you love me?

This city is an ogre squatting by the river
It gives life but it takes it away, my youth
There comes a time when you just cannot deliver
This is a fact. This is a stone cold truth
Do you love me?
I love you, handsome
But do you love me?
Yes, I love you, you are handsome
Amongst the cogs and the wires, my youth
Vanilla breath and handsome apes with girlish eyes
Dreams that roam between truth and untruth
Memories that become monstrous lies
So onward! And onward! And onward I go!
Onward! And upward! And I'm off to find love
With blue-black bracelets on my wrists and ankles
And the coins in my pocket go jingle-jangle

Do you love me?
Do you love me?
Do you love me?
Do you love me?

Sail Away

I climbed the hill, lay in the grass
A little dark-eyed girl drifted past
She said, 'All the best has come, it could not last
And the worst it has come true'

Her hands were small and fluttered up
A lamb amongst the buttercups
I pulled on my coat and buttoned it up
For the worst it had come true

Sail away, sail away
To a place where your troubles can't follow
Sail away, sail away
Save all your tears for tomorrow

The fins of the city moved toward us
And the swallows swooped and the starlings warned us
And the peril in everything it assured us
That the worst it had come true

And all my sorrows made their bed beside me
The shame, the disgrace and the brutality
And she whispered then, 'Let laughter flee
For the worst it has come true'

Dry your tears, forget why we're here
Leave all your sorrows behind you
Never lose heart, all things must pass
To a place where your troubles can't find you

She came beside me, amongst my coat
Her breath was warm against my throat
We clung to each other so very close
For the worst it had come true

Sail away, sail away
To a place where your heart will not shame you
Take my hand, through this night without end
For the worst it has come to claim you

Sail away, sail away
To a place where no one can betray you
Take my hand, through this night without end
For the worst it has come to claim you

(I'll Love You) Till the End of the World

It was a miracle I even got out of Longwood alive
This town full of men with big mouths and no guts
I mean, if you can just picture it
The whole third floor of the hotel gutted by the blast
And the street below showered in shards of broken glass
And all the drunks pouring out of the dance hall staring up at
the smoke and the flames
And the blind pencil-seller waving his stick, shouting for his
dog that lay dead on the side of the road
And me, if you can believe this, at the wheel of the car,
closing my eyes and actually praying
Not to God above, but to you, sayin'
Help me, girl
Help me, girl
I'll love you till the end of the world
With your eyes black as coal
And your long dark curls

Some things we plan
We sit and we invent and we plot and cook up
Others are works of inspiration, of poetry
And it was this genius hand that pushed me up the hotel
stairs to say my last goodbye
To a hair white as snow and a pale blue eyes saying I gotta go,
I gotta go
The bomb and the breadbasket are ready to blow
In this town of men with big mouths and no guts
The pencil-seller's dog spooked by the explosion
Leaping under my wheels as I careered out of Longwood on
my way to you
Waiting in your dress, in your dress of blue
I said thank you, girl

Thank you, girl
I'll love you till the end of the world
With your eyes black as coal
And your long dark curls

And with the horses prancing through the fields
With my knife in my jeans and the rain on the shield
I sang a song for the glory of the beauty of you, waiting for
me, in your dress of blue
Thank you, girl
Thank you, girl
I'll love you till the end of the world
With your eyes black as coal
And your long dark curls

What Can I Give You?

All my life I've failed to see
One good thing standing in front of me

And the planets gravitate around you
And the stars, the stars surround you
And the angels in heaven adore you
And the saints, the saints all stand and applaud you

What can I give you?
What can I give you in return?

Galaxies collide
They shower down around you
And I search, I stumble
And then I found you
In your room, in your crown
Reaching low, babe, reaching low down to the ground

What can I give you?
What can I give you in return?

What can I give you?
What can I give you in return?

Murder Ballads
(1996)

Song of Joy
Henry Lee
Lovely Creature
Where the Wild Roses Grow
The Curse of Millhaven
The Kindness of Strangers
Crow Jane
O'Malley's Bar

The Ballad of Robert Moore and Betty Coltrane
There is a Light
Time Jesum Transeuntum Et Non Revertentum

Song of Joy

Have mercy on me, sir
Allow me to impose on you
I have no place to stay
And my bones are cold right through
I will tell you a story
Of a man and his family
And I swear that it is true

Ten years ago I met a girl named Joy
She was a sweet and happy thing
Her eyes were bright blue jewels
And we were married in the spring
I had no idea what happiness a little love could bring
Or what life had in store
But all things move toward their end
All things move toward their end
Of that you can be sure

La la la la la la la la la la
La la la la la la la la la la

Then one morning I awoke to find her weeping
And for many days to follow
She grew so sad and lonely
Became Joy in name only
Within her breast there launched an unnamed sorrow
And a dark and grim force set sail
Farewell happy fields
Where joy forever dwells
Hail horrors hail

Was it an act of contrition or some awful premonition
As if she saw into the heart of her final blood-soaked night
Those lunatic eyes, that hungry kitchen knife
Ah, I see, sir, that I have your attention!
Well, could it be?
How often I've asked that question
Well, then in quick succession
We had babies, one, two, three

We called them Hilda, Hattie and Holly
They were their mother's children
Their eyes were bright blue jewels
And they were quiet as a mouse
There was no laughter in the house
No, not from Hilda, Hattie or Holly
'No wonder,' people said, 'poor mother Joy's so melancholy'
Well, one night there came a visitor to our little home
I was visiting a sick friend
I was a doctor then
Joy and the girls were on their own

La la la la la la la la la la
La la la la la la la la la la

Joy had been bound with electrical tape
In her mouth a gag
She'd been stabbed repeatedly
And stuffed into a sleeping bag
In their very cots my girls were robbed of their lives
Method of murder much the same as my wife's
Method of murder much the same as my wife's
It was midnight when I arrived home
Said to the police on the telephone
Someone's taken four innocent lives

They never caught the man
He's still on the loose
It seems he has done many many more
Quotes John Milton on the walls in the victim's blood
The police are investigating at tremendous cost
In my house he wrote, *'Red right hand'*
That, I'm told, is from *Paradise Lost*
The wind round here gets wicked cold
But my story is nearly told
I fear the morning will bring quite a frost

And so I've left my home
I drift from land to land
I am upon your step and you are a family man
Outside the vultures wheel
The wolves howl, the serpents hiss
And to extend this small favour, friend
Would be the sum of earthly bliss
Do you reckon me a friend?
The sun to me is dark
And silent as the moon
Do you, sir, have a room?
Are you beckoning me in?

La la la la la la la la la la
La la la la la la la la la la
La la la la la la la la la la
La la la la la la la la la la

Henry Lee

Get down, get down, little Henry Lee
And stay all night with me
You won't find a girl in this damn world
That will compare with me
And the wind did howl and the wind did blow
La la la la la
La la la la lee
A little bird lit down on Henry Lee

I can't get down and I won't get down
And stay all night with thee
For the girl I have in that merry green land
I love far better than thee
And the wind did howl and the wind did blow
La la la la la
La la la la lee
A little bird lit down on Henry Lee

She leaned herself against a fence
Just for a kiss or two
And with a little pen-knife held in her hand
She plugged him through and through
And the wind did roar and the wind did moan
La la la la la
La la la la lee
A little bird lit down on Henry Lee

Come take him by his lily-white hands
Come take him by his feet
And throw him in this deep deep well
Which is more than one hundred feet

And the wind did howl and the wind did blow
La la la la la
La la la la lee
A little bird lit down on Henry Lee

Lie there, lie there, little Henry Lee
'Til the flesh drops from your bones
For the girl you have in that merry green land
Can wait for ever for you to come home
And the wind did howl and the wind did moan
La la la la la
La la la la lee
A little bird lit down on Henry Lee

Lovely Creature

There she stands, this lovely creature
There she stands, there she stands
With her hair full of ribbons
And green gloves on her hands

So I asked this lovely creature
Yes, I asked. Yes, I asked
Would she walk with me a while
Through this night so fast

She took my hand, this lovely creature
'Yes,' she said. 'Yes,' she said
'Yes, I'll walk with you a while'
It was a joyful man she led

Over hills, this lovely creature
Over mountains, over ranges
By great pyramids and sphinxes
We met drifters and strangers

O the sands, my lovely creature
And the mad, moaning winds
At night the deserts writhed
With diabolical things

Through the night, through the night
The wind lashed and it whipped me
When I got home, my lovely creature
She was no longer with me

Somewhere she lies, this lovely creature
Beneath the slow drifting sands
With her hair full of ribbons
And green gloves on her hands

Where the Wild Roses Grow

They call me The Wild Rose
But my name was Elisa Day
Why they call me it I do not know
For my name was Elisa Day

From the first day I saw her I knew that she was the one
As she stared in my eyes and smiled
For her lips were the colour of the roses
That grew down the river, all bloody and wild

When he knocked on my door and entered the room
My trembling subsided in his sure embrace
He would be my first man, and with a careful hand
He wiped at the tears that ran down my face

They call me The Wild Rose
But my name was Elisa Day
Why they call me it I do not know
For my name was Elisa Day

On the second day I brought her a flower
She was more beautiful than any woman I'd seen
I said, 'Do you know where the wild roses grow
So sweet and scarlet and free?'

On the second day he came with a single red rose
Said, 'Will you give me your loss and your sorrow?'
I nodded my head, as I lay on the bed
He said, 'If I show you the roses, will you follow?'

They call me The Wild Rose
But my name was Elisa Day
Why they call me it I do not know
For my name was Elisa Day

On the third day he took me to the river
He showed me the roses and we kissed
And the last thing I heard was a muttered word
As he stood smiling above me with a rock in his fist

On the last day I took her where the wild roses grow
And she lay on the bank, the wind light as a thief
As I kissed her goodbye, I said, 'All beauty must die'
And lent down and planted a rose between her teeth

They call me The Wild Rose
But my name was Elisa Day
Why they call me it I do not know
For my name was Elisa Day

The Curse of Millhaven

I live in a town called Millhaven
And it's small and it's mean and it's cold
But if you come around just as the sun goes down
You can watch the whole town turn to gold
It's around about then that I used to go a-roaming
Singing La la la la, la la la lie
All God's children, they all gotta die

My name is Loretta but I prefer Lottie
I'm closing in on my fifteenth year
And if you think you have seen a pair of eyes more green
Then you sure didn't see them round here
My hair is yellow and I'm always a-combing
La la la la, la la la lie
Mama often told me, we all have to die

You must have heard about the Curse of Millhaven
How last Christmas Bill Blake's little boy didn't come home
They found him next week in One Mile Creek
His head bashed in and his pockets full of stones
Well, just imagine the wailing and moaning
La la la la, la la la lie
Even little Billy Blake, he had to die.

Then Professor O'Rye from Millhaven High
Found nailed to his door his prize-winning terrier
The next day the old fool brought little Biko to school
And we all had to watch as he buried her
His eulogy to Biko had all the tears a-flowing
La la la la, la la la lie
Even God's little creatures, they have to die

Our little town fell into a state of shock
A lot of people were saying things that made little sense
Then the next thing you know the head of Handyman Joe
Was found in the fountain of the Mayor's residence
Foul play can really get a small town going
La la la la, la la la lie
All God's children, all have to die

Then, in a cruel twist of fate, old Mrs Colgate
Was stabbed but the job was not complete
The last thing she said before the cops pronounced her
 dead
Was, 'My killer is Loretta and she lives across the street!'
Twenty cops burst through my door without even phoning
La la la la, la la la lie
The young ones, the old ones, they all gotta die

Yes, it is I, Lottie, the Curse of Millhaven
I've struck horror in the heart of this town
Like my eyes ain't green and my hair ain't yellow
It's more like the other way around
I gotta a pretty little mouth underneath all the foaming
La la la la, la la la lie
Sooner or later we all gotta die

Since I was no bigger than a weevil they've been saying I was
 evil
That if 'bad' was a boot then I'd fit it
That I'm a wicked young lady, but I've been trying hard
 lately
O fuck it! I'm a monster! I admit it!
It makes me so mad, my blood really starts a-going
La la la la, la la la lie
Mama always told me that we all gotta die

Yeah, I drowned the Blakey kid, stabbed Mrs Colgate, I admit
Did the handyman with his circular saw in his garden shed
But I never crucified little Biko, that was two junior high
school psychos
Stinky Bohoon and his friend with the pumpkin-sized head
I'll sing to the lot, now you got me going
La la la la, la la la lie
All God's children have all gotta die

There were all of the others, all our sisters and brothers
You assumed were accidents, best forgotten
Recall the children who broke through the ice on Lake Tahoo?
Everyone assumed the 'Warning' signs had followed them to
the bottom
Well, they're underneath the house where I do quite a bit of
stowing
La la la la, la la la lie
Even twenty little chilren, they had to die

And the fire of '91 that razed the Bella Vista slum
There was the biggest shit-fight this country's ever seen
Insurance companies ruined, landlords getting sued
All 'cause of a wee little girl with a can of gasoline
Those flames really roared when the wind started blowing
La la la la, la la la lie
Rich man, poor man, all got to die

Well, I confessed to all these crimes and then they put me on
trial
I was laughing when they took me away
Off to the asylum in an old Black Maria
It ain't home, but you know, it's fucking better than jail
It ain't such a bad old place to have a home in
La la la la, la la la lie
All God's children, they all gotta die

Now I got shrinks that will not rest with their endless
Rorschach tests
I keep telling them they're out to get me
They asked me if I feel remorse and I answer, 'Why of
course!
There is so much more I could have done if they'd let me!'
So it's Rorschach and Prozac and everything is groovy
Singing La la la la, la la la lie
All God's children have all gotta die
La la la la, la la la lie
I'm happy as a lark and everything is fine
Singing La la la la, la la la lie
Yeah, everything is groovy and everything is fine
Singing La la la la, la la la lie
All God's children, they all gotta die

The Kindness of Strangers

They found Mary Bellows ’cuffed to the bed
With a rag in her mouth and a bullet in her head
O poor Mary Bellows

She’d grown up hungry, she’d grown up poor
So she left her home in Arkansas
O poor Mary Bellows

She wanted to see the deep blue sea
She drove across Tennessee
O poor Mary Bellows

She met a man along the way
He introduced himself as Richard Slade
O poor Mary Bellows

Poor Mary thought that she might die
When she saw the ocean for the first time
O poor Mary Bellows

She checked into a cheap little place
Richard Slade carried in her old suitcase
O poor Mary Bellows

‘I’m a good girl, sir,’ she said to him
‘I couldn’t possibly permit you in’
O poor Mary Bellows

Slade tipped his hat and winked his eye
And turned away without goodbye
O poor Mary Bellows

She sat on her bed and thought of home
With the sea breeze whistling, all alone
O poor Mary Bellows

In hope and loneliness she crossed the floor
And undid the latch on the front door
O poor Mary Bellows

They found her next day 'cuffed to the bed
A rag in her mouth and a bullet in her head
O poor Mary Bellows

So mothers keep your girls at home
Don't let them journey out alone
Tell them this world is full of danger
And to shun the company of strangers
O poor Mary Bellows
O poor Mary Bellows

Crow Jane

Crow Jane, Crow Jane, Crow Jane
Horrors in her head
That her tongue dare not name
Lived all alone by the river
The rolling rivers of pain
Crow Jane, Crow Jane, Crow Jane, ah hah huh

There is one shining eye on a hard-hat
Company closed down the mine
Winking on the waters they came
Twenty hard-hats, twenty eyes
In her clapboard shack
Just six foot by five
They killed all her whiskey
Poured their pistols dry
Crow Jane, Crow Jane, Crow Jane, ah hah huh

Seems you've remembered
How to sleep, how to sleep
The house dogs are in your turnips
And your yard dogs are running all over the streets
Crow Jane, Crow Jane, Crow Jane, ah hah huh

'O Mr Smith and Mr Wesson
Why you close up shop so late?'
Just fitted out a girl who looked like a bird
Measured .32, .44, .38
Asked that gal which road she was taking
Said she was walking the road of hate
But she hopped on a coal-trolley up to New Haven
Population: 48
Crow Jane, Crow Jane, Crow Jane, ah hah huh

Your guns are drunk and smoking
They have followed you to the gate
Laughing all the way back from the new town
Population, now: 28
Crow Jane, Crow Jane, Crow Jane, ah hah huh

O'Malley's Bar

I am tall and I am thin
Of an enviable height
And I've been known to be quite handsome
From a certain angle and in a certain light

Well, I entered into O'Malley's
Said, 'O'Malley, I have a thirst'
O'Malley merely smiled at me
Said, 'You wouldn't be the first'

I knocked on the bar and pointed
To a bottle on the shelf
And as O'Malley poured me out a drink
I sniffed and crossed myself

My hand decided that the time was nigh
And for a moment it slipped from view
And when it returned, it fairly burned
With confidence anew

Well, the thunder from my steely fist
Made all the glasses jangle
When I shot him, I was so handsome
It was the light, it was the angle

Huh! Hmmmmm

'Neighbours!' I cried. 'Friends!' I screamed
I banged my fist upon the bar
'I bear no grudge against you!'
And my dick felt long and hard

'I am the man for which no God waits
For which the whole world yearns
I'm marked by darkness and by blood
And one thousand powder-burns'

Well, you know those fish with the swollen lips
That clean the ocean floor?
When I looked at poor O'Malley's wife
That is exactly what I saw

I jammed the barrel under her chin
And her face looked raw and vicious
Her head it landed in the sink
With all the dirty dishes

Her little daughter Siobhan
Pulled beers from dusk 'til dawn
And amongst the townfolk, she was a bit of a joke
But she pulled the best beers in town

I swooped magnificent upon her
As she sat shivering in her grief
Like the Madonna painted on the church-house wall
In whale's blood and banana leaf

Her throat it crumbled in my fist
And I spun heroically around
To see Caffrey rising from his chair
I shot that motherfucker down

Mmmmmmmmm, yeah yeah yeah

'I have no free will,' I sang
As I flew about the murder
Mrs Richard Holmes, she screamed
You really should have heard her

I sang and I laughed, I howled and I wept
I panted like a pup
I blew a hole in Mrs Richard Holmes
And her husband, he stood up

And he screamed, 'You are an evil man'
And I paused a while to wonder
'If I have no free will then how can I
Be morally culpable, I wonder'

I shot Richard Holmes in the stomach
And gingerly he sat down
And he whispered weirdly, 'No offence'
And lay upon the ground

'None taken,' I replied to him
With which he gave a little cough
With blazing wings I neatly aimed
And blew his head completely off

I've lived in this town for thirty years
And to no one am I a stranger
And I put new bullets in my gun
Chamber upon chamber

And when I turned my gun on the bird-like Mr Brookes
I thought of Saint Francis and his sparrows
And as I shot down the youthful Richardson
It was Sebastian I thought of, and his arrows

Hhhhhhhhhhhh
Mmmmmmmmm

I said, 'I want to introduce myself
And I am glad that you all came'
And I leapt upon the bar
And shouted out my name

Well, Jerry Bellows, he hugged his stool
Closed his eyes and shrugged and laughed
And with an ashtray as big as a fucking big brick
I split his head in half

His blood spilled across the bar
Like a steaming scarlet brook
And I knelt at its edge on the counter
Wiped the tears away and looked

Well, the light in there was blinding
Full of God and ghosts and truth
I smiled at Henry Davenport
Who made no attempt to move

Well, from the position I was standing
The strangest thing I ever saw
The bullet entered through the top of his chest
And blew his bowels out on the floor

Well, I floated down the counter
Showing no remorse
I shot a hole in Kathleen Carpenter
Recently divorced

But remorse I felt and remorse I had
It clung to every thing
From the raven hair upon my head
To the feathers on my wings

Remorse squeezed my hand in its fraudulent claw
With its golden hairless chest
And I glided through the bodies
And killed the fat man Vincent West

Who sat quietly in his chair
A man become a child
And I raised the gun up to his head
Executioner-style

He made no attempt to resist
So fat and dull and lazy
'Do you know I live in your street?' I cried
And he looked at me as though I were crazy

'O,' he said, 'I had no idea'
And he grew as quiet as a mouse
And the roar of the pistol when it went off
Near blew the hat right off the house

Well, I caught my eye in the mirror
And gave it a long and loving inspection
'There stands some kind of man,' I roared
And there did, in the reflection

My hair combed back like a raven's wing
My muscles hard and tight
And curling from the business end of my gun
Was a query-mark of cordite

Well, I spun to the left, I spun to the right
And I spun to the left again
'Fear me! Fear me!'
But no one did 'cause they were dead

Huh! Hmmmmmmmm

And then there were the police sirens wailing
And a bull-horn squelched and blared
'Drop your weapon and come out
With your hands held in the air'

Well, I checked the chamber of my gun
Saw I had one final bullet left
My hand, it looked almost human
As I held it to my head

'Drop your weapon and come out!
Keep your hands above your head!'
Well, I had one long hard think about dying
And did exactly what they said

There must have been fifty cops out there
In a circle around O'Malley's bar
'Don't shoot,' I cried. 'I'm a man unarmed!'
So they put me in their car

And they sped me away from that terrible scene
And I glanced out of the window
Saw O'Malley's bar, saw the cops and the cars
And started counting on my fingers

Aaaaaaaaah one, aaaaaaaah two, aaaaaah three, aaaah four
O'Malley's bar, O'Malley's bar

The Ballad of Robert Moore and Betty Coltrane

There was a thick-set man with frog-eyes who was standing at
the door
And a little bald man with wing-nut ears was waiting in the car
Well, Robert Moore passed the frog-eyed man as he walked
into the bar
And Betty Coltrane she jumped under her table

'What's your pleasure?' asked the barman, he had a face like
boiled meat
'There's a girl called Betty Coltrane that I have come to see'
'But I ain't seen that girl round here for more than a week'
And Betty Coltrane she hid beneath the table

Well, then in came a sailor with mermaids tattooed on his
arms
Followed by the man with wing-nut ears who was waiting in
the car
Well, Robert Moore sensed trouble, he'd seen it coming from
afar
And Betty Coltrane she gasped beneath the table

Well, the sailor said, 'I'm looking for my wife! They call her
Betty Coltrane'
And the frog-eyed man said, 'That can't be! That's my wife's
maiden name!'
And the man with the wing-nut ears said, 'Hey, I married her
back in Spain'
And Betty Coltrane crossed herself beneath the table

Well, Robert Moore stepped up and said, 'That woman is my wife'
And he drew a silver pistol and a wicked Bowie knife
And he shot the man with the wing-nut ears straight between the eyes
And Betty Coltrane she moaned under the table

Well, the frog-eyed man jumped at Robert Moore who stabbed him in the chest
As Mr Frog-eyes died, he said, 'Betty, you're the girl that I loved best'
Then the sailor pulled a razor and Robert blasted him to bits
And said, 'Betty, I know you're under the table!'

'Well, have no fear' said Robert Moore 'I do not want to hurt you
Never a woman did I love near half as much as you
You are the blessed sun to me, girl, and you are the sacred moon'
And Betty shot his legs out from under the table

Well, Robert Moore went down heavy with a crash upon the floor
And over to his thrashing body Betty Coltrane she did crawl
She put the gun to the back of his head and pulled the trigger once more
And blew his brains out all over the table

Well, Betty stood up and shook her head and waved the smoke away
Said, 'I'm sorry, Mr Barman, to leave your place this way'
As she emptied out their wallets, she said, 'I'll collect my severance pay'
Then she winked and threw a dollar on the table

There is a Light

Hey there, Sugar, where ya gunna go
I'm going downtown, Daddy-O
What ya gunna do when you get there, girl?
I'm gunna get messed up in a God-shaped hole
Hey, Mr Hophead, what ya gunna do?
I'm going downtown for some bad ju-ju
Ya going downtown too, Mr Gigolo?
Damn right I am, Daddy-O

There is a light that shines over this city tonight
There is a light that shines over this city tonight
Let it shine

O Mr High-Roller, where you gunna go?
Where the real high-rolling rollers roll real dough
Hey, Mr Killer-Man, what you gunna do?
Me and Mr Death are going downtown too
Ain't there one God-fearing citizen about?
They're holed up and they ain't coming out
What about Mr Preacher to forgive our sins?
Not that carrion crow with blood on his chin
And Mr Politician, can't he lend a hand?
He's too busy sucking on the guts of this town
And what about God and this Armageddon?
He's all blissed-out, man, up in Heaven
Ain't there nowhere to run, ain't there nowhere to go?
Ain't there nowhere to run, ain't there nowhere to go?
Ain't there nowhere to run, ain't there nowhere to go?
Ain't there nowhere to run, ain't there nowhere to go?
Yeah, look to the sky, Daddy-O

There is a light that shines over this city tonight
There is a light that shines over this city tonight
Let it shine, let it shine, let it shine

What are the little kids gunna do, man?
The little kids are all standing around
What are the kids doing, do you know?
They are looking to the sky, Daddy-O

Time Jesum Transeuntum Et Non Revertentum

We were called to the forest and we went down
A wind blew warm and eloquent
We were searching for the secrets of the universe
And we rounded up demons
And forced them to tell us what it all meant
We tied them to trees and broke them down one by one
On a scrap of paper they wrote these words
And as we read them the sun broke through the trees
'Dread the passage of Jesus for He will not return'
Then we headed back to our world and left the forest behind
Our hearts singing with all the knowledge of love
But somewhere, somehow we lost the message along the way
And when we got home we bought ourselves a house
And we bought a car that we did not use
And we bought a cage and two singing birds
And at night we'd sit and listen to the canaries' song
For we'd both run right out of words
Now the stars they are all angled wrong
And the sun and the moon refuse to burn
But I remember a message in a demon's hand
Dread the passage of Jesus for He does not return

The Boatman's Call
(1997)

Into My Arms
Lime-Tree Arbour
People Ain't No Good
Brompton Oratory
There is a Kingdom
(Are You) the One that I've Been Waiting For?
Where Do We Go Now But Nowhere?
West Country Girl
Black Hair
Idiot Prayer
Far From Me
Green Eyes

Little Empty Boat
Come Into My Sleep
Right Now, I am A-Roaming
Babe, I Got You Bad
The Bridle Path
Wife
Opium Tea
The Sweetest Embrace
Little Water Song
Still Your Face Comes Shining Through
Sweet Little Sleep
Sheep May Safely Graze

Into My Arms

I don't believe in an interventionist God
But I know, darling, that you do
But if I did I would kneel down and ask Him
Not to intervene when it came to you
Not to touch a hair on your head
To leave you as you are
And if He felt He had to direct you
Then direct you into my arms

Into my arms, O Lord
Into my arms, O Lord
Into my arms, O Lord
Into my arms

And I don't believe in the existence of angels
But looking at you I wonder if that's true
But if I did I would summon them together
And ask them to watch over you
To each burn a candle for you
To make bright and clear your path
And to walk, like Christ, in grace and love
And guide you into my arms

Into my arms, O Lord
Into my arms, O Lord
Into my arms, O Lord
Into my arms

But I believe in Love
And I know that you do too
And I believe in some kind of path
That we can walk down, me and you

So keep your candles burning
And make her journey bright and pure
That she will keep returning
Always and evermore

Into my arms, O Lord
Into my arms, O Lord
Into my arms, O Lord
Into my arms

Lime-Tree Arbour

The boatman calls from the lake
A lone loon dives upon the water
I put my hand over hers
Down in the lime-tree arbour

The wind in the trees is whispering
Whispering low that I love her
She puts her hand over mine
Down in the lime-tree arbour

Through every breath that I breathe
And every place I go
There is a hand that protects me
And I do love her so

There will always be suffering
It flows through life like water
I put my hand over hers
Down in the lime-tree arbour

The boatman he has gone
And the loons have flown for cover
She puts her hand over mine
Down in the lime-tree arbour

Through every word that I speak
And every thing I know
There is a hand that protects me
And I do love her so

People Ain't No Good

People just ain't no good
I think that's well understood
You can see it everywhere you look
People just ain't no good

We were married under cherry trees
Under blossom we made our vows
All the blossoms come sailing down
Through the streets and through the playgrounds

The sun would stream on the sheets
Awoken by the morning bird
We'd buy the Sunday newspapers
And never read a single word

People they ain't no good
People they ain't no good
People they ain't no good

Seasons came, seasons went
The winter stripped the blossoms bare
A different tree now lines the streets
Shaking its fists in the air

The winter slammed us like a fist
The windows rattling in the gales
To which she drew the curtains
Made out of her wedding veils

People they ain't no good
People they ain't no good
People they ain't no good

To our love send a dozen white lilies
To our love send a coffin of wood
To our love let all the pink-eyed pigeons coo
That people they just ain't no good
To our love send back all the letters
To our love a valentine of blood
To our love let all the jilted lovers cry
That people they just ain't no good

It ain't that in their hearts they're bad
They can comfort you, some even try
They nurse you when you're ill of health
They bury you when you go and die
It ain't that in their hearts they're bad
They'd stick by you if they could
But that's just bullshit, baby
People just ain't no good

People they ain't no good
People they ain't no good
People they ain't no good
People they ain't no good

Brompton Oratory

Up those stone steps I climb
Hail this joyful day's return
Into its great shadowed vault I go
Hail the Pentecostal morn

The reading is from Luke 24
Where Christ returns to his loved ones
I look at the stone apostles
Think that it's all right for some

And I wish that I was made of stone
So that I would not have to see
A beauty impossible to define
A beauty impossible to believe

A beauty impossible to endure
The blood imparted in little sips
The smell of you still on my hands
As I bring the cup up to my lips

No God up in the sky
No Devil beneath the sea
Could do the job that you did
Of bringing me to my knees

Outside I sit on the stone steps
With nothing much to do
Forlorn and exhausted, baby
By the absence of you

There is a Kingdom

Just like a bird that sings up the sun
In a dawn so very dark
Such is my faith for you
Such is my faith
And all the world's darkness can't swallow up
A single spark
Such is my love for you
Such is my love

There is a kingdom
There is a king
And He lives without
And He lives within

The starry heavens above me
The moral law within
So the world appears
So the world appears
This day so sweet
It will never come again
So the world appears
Through this mist of tears

There is a kingdom
There is a king
And He lives without
And He lives within
And He is everything

(Are You) the One that I've Been Waiting For?

I've felt you coming, girl, as you drew near
I knew you'd find me, 'cause I longed you here
Are you my destiny? Is this how you'll appear?
Wrapped in a coat with tears in your eyes?
Well take that coat, babe, and throw it on the floor
Are you the one that I've been waiting for?

As you've been moving surely toward me
My soul has comforted and assured me
That in time my heart it will reward me
And that all will be revealed
So I've sat and I've watched an ice-age thaw
Are you the one that I've been waiting for?

Out of sorrow entire worlds have been built
Out of longing great wonders have been willed
They're only little tears, darling, let them spill
And lay your head upon my shoulder
Outside my window the world has gone to war
Are you the one that I've been waiting for?

O we will know, won't we?
The stars will explode in the sky
O but they don't, do they?
Stars have their moment and then they die

There's a man who spoke wonders though I've never met him
He said, 'He who seeks finds and who knocks will be let in'
I think of you in motion and just how close you are getting
And how every little thing anticipates you
All down my veins my heart-strings call
Are you the one that I've been waiting for?

Where Do We Go Now But Nowhere?

I remember a girl so very well
The carnival drums all mad in the air
Grim reapers and skeletons and a missionary bell
O where do we go now but nowhere

In a colonial hotel we fucked up the sun
And then we fucked it down again
Well, the sun comes up and the sun goes down
Going round and around to nowhere

The kitten that padded and purred on my lap
Now swipes at my face with the paw of a bear
I turn the other cheek and you lay into that
O where do we go now but nowhere

O wake up, my love, my lover, wake up
O wake up, my love, my lover, wake up

Across clinical benches with nothing to talk
Breathing tea and biscuits and the Serenity Prayer
While the bones of our child crumble like chalk
O where do we go now but nowhere

I remember a girl so bold and so bright
Loose-limbed and laughing and brazen and bare
Sits gnawing her knuckles in the chemical light
O where do we go now but nowhere

You come for me now with a cake that you've made
Ravaged avenger with a clip in your hair
Full of glass and bleach and my old razor blades
O where do we go now but nowhere

O wake up, my love, my lover, wake up
O wake up, my love, my lover, wake up

If they'd give me my clothes back then I could go home
From this fresh, this clean, antiseptic air
Behind the locked gates an old donkey moans
O where do we go now but nowhere

Around the duck pond we grimly mope
Gloomily and mournfully we go round again
And one more doomed time and without much hope
Going round and around to nowhere

From the balcony we watched the carnival band
The crack of the drum a little child did scare
I can still feel his tiny fingers pressed in my hand
O where do we go now but nowhere

If I could relive one day of my life
If I could relive just a single one
You on the balcony, my future wife
O who could have known, but no one

O wake up, my love, my lover, wake up
O wake up, my love, my lover, wake up

West Country Girl

With a crooked smile and a heart-shaped face
Comes from the West Country where the birds sing bass
She's got a house-big heart where we all live
And plead and counsel and forgive
Her widow's peak, her lips I've kissed
Her glove of bones at her wrist
That I have held in my hand
Her Spanish fly and her monkey gland
Her Godly body and its fourteen stations
That I have embraced, her palpitations
Her unborn baby crying, 'Mummy'
Amongst the rubble of her body
Her lovely lidded eyes I've sipped
Her fingernails, all pink and chipped
Her accent which I'm told is 'broad'
That I have heard and has been poured
Into my human heart and filled me
With love, up to the brim, and killed me
And rebuilt me back anew
With something to look forward to
Well, who could ask much more than that?
A West Country girl with a big fat cat?
That looks into her eyes of green
And meows, 'He loves you,' then meows again

Black Hair

Last night my kisses were banked in black hair
And in my bed, my lover, her hair was midnight black
And all her mystery dwelled within her black hair
And her black hair framed a happy heart-shaped face
And heavy-hooded eyes inside her black hair
Shined at me from the depths of her hair of deepest black
While my fingers pushed into her straight black hair
Pulling her black hair back from her happy heart-shaped face
To kiss her milk-white throat, a dark curtain of black hair
Smothered me, my lover with her beautiful black hair
The smell of it is heavy. It is charged with life
On my fingers the smell of her deep black hair
Full of all my whispered words, her black hair
And wet with tears and goodbyes, her hair of deepest black
All my tears cried against her milk-white throat
Hidden behind the curtain of her beautiful black hair
As deep as ink and black, black as the deepest sea
The smell of her black hair upon my pillow
Where her head and all its black hair did rest
Today she took a train to the West
Today she took a train to the West
Today she took a train to the West

Idiot Prayer

They're taking me down, my friend
And as they usher me off to my end
Will I bid you adieu?
Or will I be seeing you soon?
If what they say around here is true
Then we'll meet again
Me and you

My time is at hand, my dove
They're gunna pass me to that house above
Is Heaven just for victims, dear?
Where only those in pain go?
Well, it takes two to tango
We will meet again, my love
I know

If you're in Heaven, then you'll forgive me, dear
Because that's what they do up there
But if you're in Hell, then what can I say
You probably deserved it anyway
I guess I'm gunna find out any day
For we will meet again
And there'll be Hell to pay

Your face comes to me from the depths, dear
Your silent mouth mouths, 'Yes,' dear
Dark red and big with blood
They're gunna shut me down, my love
They're gunna launch me into the stars
Well, all things come to pass
Yeah, Glory Hallelujah

This prayer is for you, my love
Sent on the wings of a dove
An idiot prayer of empty words
Love, dear, is strictly for the birds
We each get what we deserve
My little snow white dove
Rest assured

Far From Me

For you, dear, I was born
For you I was raised up
For you I've lived and for you I will die
For you I am dying now
You were my mad little lover
In a world where everybody fucks everybody else over
You who are so
Far from me
So far from me
Way across some cold neurotic sea
Far from me

I would talk to you of all manner of things
With a smile you would reply
Then the sun would leave your pretty face
And you'd retreat from the front of your eyes
I keep hearing that you're doing your best
I hope your heart beats happy in your infant breast
You are so far from me
Far from me
Far from me

There is no knowledge but I know it
There's nothing to learn from that vacant voice
That sails to me across the line
From the ridiculous to the sublime
It's good to hear you're doing so well
But really, can't you find somebody else that you can ring and
tell?
Did you ever care for me?
Were you ever there for me?
So far from me

You told me you'd stick by me
Through the thick and through the thin
Those were your very words
My fair-weathered friend
You were my brave-hearted lover
At the first taste of trouble went running back to mother
So far from me
Far from me
Suspended in your bleak and fishless sea
Far from me
Far from me

Green Eyes

Kiss me again, re-kiss me and kiss me
Slip your frigid hands beneath my shirt
This useless old fucker with his twinkling cunt
Doesn't care if he gets hurt

Green eyes, green eyes
Green eyes, green eyes

If it were but a matter of faith
If it were measured in petitions and prayer
She would materialize, all fleshed out
But it is not, nor do I care

Green eyes, green eyes
Green eyes, green eyes

So hold me and hold me, don't tell me your name
This morning will be wiser than this evening is
Then leave me to my enemied dreams
And be quiet as you are leaving, Miss

Green eyes, green eyes
Green eyes, green eyes

Little Empty Boat

You found me at some party
You thought I'd understand
You barrelled over to me
With a drink in each hand
I respect your beliefs, girl
And I consider you a friend
But I've already been born once
I don't wanna be born again
Your knowledge is impressive
And your argument is good
But I am the resurrection, babe
And you're standing on my foot

But my little boat is empty
It don't go!
And my oar is broken
It don't row, row, row!
My little boat is empty
It don't go!
And my oar is broken
It don't row, row, row!

Your tiny little face
Keeps yapping in the gloom
Seven steps behind me
With your dustpan and broom
I can't help but imagine you
All postured and prone
But there's a little guy on my shoulder
Says I should go home alone

But you keep leaning in on me
And you're looking pretty pissed
That grave you've dug between your legs
Is hard to resist

But my little boat is empty
It don't go!
And my oar is broken
It don't row, row, row!
My little boat is empty
It don't go!
And my oar is broken
It don't row, row, row!

Give to God what belongs to God
And give the rest to me
Tell our gracious host to fuck himself
It's time for us to leave

But my little boat is empty
It don't go!
And my oar is broken
It don't row, row, row!
My little boat is empty
It don't go!
And my oar is broken
It don't row, row, row!

Come Into My Sleep

Now that mountains of meaningless words
And oceans divide us
And we each have our own set of stars
To comfort and guide us
Come into my sleep
Come into my sleep
Dry your eyes and do not weep
Come into my sleep

Swim to me through the deep blue sea
Upon the scattered stars set sail
Fly to me through this love-lit night
From one thousand miles away
And come into my sleep
Come into my sleep
As midnight nears and shadows creep
Come into my sleep

Bind my dreams up in your tangled hair
For I am sick at heart, my dear
Bind my dreams up in your tangled hair
For all sorrow it will pass, my dear

Take your accusations, your recriminations
And toss them into the ocean blue
Leave your regrets and impossible longings
And scatter them across the sky behind you
And come into my sleep
Come into my sleep
For my soul to comfort and keep
Come into my sleep
Dry your eyes and come into my sleep

Right Now, I am A-Roaming

When I get home
I'm gunna clean up my house
When I get home
I'm gunna kick out that mouse
When I get home
I'm gunna put things in order
But right now, right right now
Right now, I am a-roaming

When I get home
I'm gunna make that call
When I get home
I'm gunna talk it through
When I get home
I'm gunna straighten it out
But right now, right now
Right now, I am a-roaming

When I get home
I'm gunna give up the booze
When I get home
I'm gunna eat some food
When I get home
I'm gunna kick them drugs
But right now, right now
Right now, I am a-roaming

When I get home
I'm gunna call my mother
When I get home
I'm gunna cook her some dinner

When I get home
I'm gunna invite my brothers
But right now, right right now
Right now, I am a-roaming

When I get home
I'm gunna see my little boy
When I get home
I'm gunna buy him a toy
When I get home
He's gunna jump for joy
But right now, right right now
Right now, I am a-roaming

When I get home
I'm gunna unpack my bags
When I get home
I'm gunna wash these dirty rags
When I get home
I'm gunna pack them up again
And I'm gunna go, I'm gunna go
Right back a-roaming

Babe, I Got You Bad

Babe, I got you bad
Dreaming blood-wet dreams
Only madmen have
Babe, I got you bad
I wish to God I never had
It makes me so damn sad
O babe, I got you bad
Yeah babe, I got you bad

I long for your kiss
The turn of your mouth
Your body is a long thing
Heading South
And I don't know what I'm talking about
All my words have gone mad
O babe, I got you bad

The seasons have gone wrong
And I lay me down in a bed of snow
Darling, since you been gone
My hands, they don't know where to go
And all my teeth are bared
I got you so much I'm scared
O baby, I got you bad

With a sweep of my hand
I undid all the plans
That exploded the moment I kissed you
On your small hot mouth
And your caramel limbs
Which are hymns to the glory that is you

Look at me darling, it's sad sad sad
Look at me darling, it's sad sad sad
Baby, I got you bad

Smoke billowing from the bridges
And the rivers we swam in are boiling
My hands are reaching for you everywhere
But you're not there, or you're recoiling
A weary moon dangles from a cloud
O honey, I know it's not allowed
To say I got you bad

The Bridle Path

Luck kissed my brow and held me close
Said, 'I can no longer stay
My brother will watch over you
While I'm gone away'

'You two will get on fine,' he said
But he really did not convince
The sun turned grey as he rode away
And I haven't seen him since

'I didn't catch your name,' I said
Luck's brother answered so
'My name is Love,' he said to me
'I'm sad to see my brother go'

His teeth were straight and pearly white
His eyes the clearest blue
And when he spoke a second time
His voice was rich and smooth

'Look yonder,' said Love and pointed
Then gave a winning little laugh
I saw the prettiest young thing, with a wedding ring
Walk down the bridle path

Wife

Here she comes, my wife
See her down on the street
Well, yeah, she's mine, supine
Or up on her feet

Yeah, here she comes
Through the dog-breath heat
With her concertina spine
And her ballerina feet

Under a punishing sun
Under a red and green umbrella
Call her name and beat the drum
Through the condominiums and the favelas

God is gone. We got to get a new one
Not lock Him down in cathedrals and cages
I found the eternal woman
The fire that leapt from Solomon's pages

O baby, here she comes
My righteous, ringless bride
She is the soul of an ailing continent
She is Latin America's pride

There she runs, through the rain
Through cities of packed dirt and bone
She's prepared to accept the burden of the world's great
pain
Provided you accept the burden of your own

Ah, here she comes
I will love her for all time
In her little, small floral skirt, so short
Defying rhythm, defying rhyme

The cats are crying like babies
Up and down the alleys
The kids are howling like cats
With not enough in their bellies

Here, she's gaily tripping through the streets
Cats and kids stop to stare
The kids all bang their guitars
They shoot their guns into the air

She don't carry no gun
Her lips are loaded up with kisses
She got kisses all around her hips
She got them criss-crossing her breasts

Keep playing that song
Don't let the band go home
I tell you God is gone
We are on our own

Yeah, here she comes
In a dress of red and yellow
Up the steps to our home
I got something to tell her

I say, I say, b-b-b-b-b-baby!
Ye-e-e-e-ah! Yea-a-a-a-h! Uh-huh!
O b-b-b-baby!
A-a-a-ah here she comes!

Opium Tea

Here I sleep the morning through
Until the call to prayer awakes me
And there is nothing to do but rise
And follow the day wherever it takes me
I stand at the window and look at the sea
Then I make me a pot of opium tea

Down at the port I watch the boats come in
Watching boats come in can do something to you
And the kids gather round with outstretched hand
And I toss them a dirham or two
And I wonder if my children are thinking of me
For I am what I am and what will be will be
I wonder if my kids are thinking of me
And I smile and I sip my opium tea

At night the sea lashes the rust red ramparts
And the shapes of hooded men move past me
And the mad moaning wind, it laughs and it laughs
At the strange lot that fate has cast me
And the cats on the rampart sing merrily
That I am what I am and what will be will be
The cats on the rampart sing merrily
And I sit and I drink my opium tea

I'm a prisoner here, I can never go home
There is nothing here to win or to lose
There are no choices needing to be made at all
Not even the choice of having to choose
I am a prisoner, yes, but I am also free
'Cause I am what I am and what will be will be
I'm a prisoner here, yes, but I'm also free
And I smile and I sip my opium tea

The Sweetest Embrace

Our time is done, my love
We've laid it all to waste
One thousand moonlit kisses
Can't sweeten this bitter taste
My desire for you is endless
And I'll love you 'til we fall
I just don't want you no more
And that's the sweetest embrace of all

To think we can find happiness
Hidden in a kiss
Ah, to think we can find happiness
That's the greatest mistake there is
There is nothing left to cling to, babe
There is nothing left to soil
I just don't want you no more
And that's the sweetest embrace of all

O where did it begin
When all we did was lose
There's nothin' left to win

So lay your weapons down
They serve no purpose in your hands
And if you wanna hold me
Then go ahead and hold me
I won't upset your plans
If it's revenge you want
Then take it, babe
Or you can walk right out the door
I just don't want you anymore
And that's the sweetest embrace of all

O where did it begin
When all we did was lose
There's nothin' left to win

It's over, babe
And it really is a shame
We are losers you and me, babe
In a rigged and crooked game
My desire for you is endless
And I love you most of all
I just don't want you no more
And that's the sweetest embrace of all

Little Water Song (with Bruno Pisek)

Under here, you just take my breath away
Under here, the water flows over my head
I can hear the little fishes

Under here whispering your most terrible name
Under here, they've given me starfish for eyes
And your head is a big red balloon

Under here, your huge hand is heavy on my chest
Ah, under here, Sir, your lovely voice retreats
And yes, you take my breath away

Look at my hair, as it waves and waves
Sir, under here, I have such pretty hair
Silver, it is, and filled with silver bubbles

And under here, my blood will be a cloud
And my dreams are made of water
And, Sir, you just take my breath away

For under here, my pretty breasts are piled high
With stones and I cannot breathe
And tiny fishes enter me

Under here, I am made ready
Under here, I am washed clean
And I glow with the greatness of my hate for you

Still Your Face Comes Shining Through

I've learned from you
A thing or two
About the fine art of peeling grapes
Down on the floor
Where I worship and adore
You up in your litter
With your ivory and apes

Still your face comes shining through
Still your face comes shining through
Still your face comes shining through
Still your face comes shining through

I light a cigarette
And try to forget
But through my window that melody sails
A lone violin
Playing some fucking thing
From Ireland or Scotland or Wales

Still your face comes shining through
Still your face comes shining through
Still your face comes shining through
Still your face comes shining through

I look at you
You look at me too
And deep in our hearts we know it
I read it the news
You weren't much of a muse
But then I weren't much of a poet

Still your face comes shining through
Still your face comes shining through
Still your face comes shining through
Still your face comes shining through

There's a language of love
That rises above
All knowledge and science and art
It doesn't take much
Just a whisper and a touch
To thoroughly demolish a heart

Still your face comes shining through
Still your face comes shining through
Still your face comes shining through
Still your face comes shining through

Sweet Little Sleep

It's sad
When your eyes look back
Seems that time
Gets tired of everyone
They say that time heals everything
But I'm still crying
You can tell them from me
That they is a liar

Sweet little sleep
Sweet little sleep
Have the years been kind to you?
Or have they broken your heart in two?
Sweet little sleep
Sweet little sleep

My friends don't come around anymore
Anyway I don't answer the door
Me, I move with the ghosts now
They say there's plenty of fish in the sea
How dare they say that to me?

Sweet little sleep
Sweet little sleep
Have the years been good to you?
Have they broken your heart in two?
Baby
Sweet little sleep

Sheep May Safely Graze

Sheep may safely graze
All the wolves have been rounded up and put to bed
Sheep may safely graze
There are only days of happiness up ahead
Sheep may safely graze, my boy
All the crocodiles have been hunted from your dreams
Sheep may safely graze
Woolly lambs are gambolling by the streams
Sheep may safely graze
All the lost children will be found in time
Sheep may safely graze, my boy, close your eyes
Your daddy is by your side

And if by chance you wake at night
And a hollow sorrow that lingers
And you grab at the tails of your dreams
But they scuttle through your fingers
All you can hear outside is the roar of a city being razed
That's just the powers that be making it safe to graze

Sheep may safely graze
The bluebirds have chased the vultures from the skies
Sheep may safely graze
The day is merely gone now and closed its eyes
Sheep may safely graze, my boy
All the fishes are leaping into the nets
Sheep may safely graze
This, my darling, is as good as it gets
Sheep may safely graze
All the lost children will be found in time
Sheep may safely graze, my boy, close your eyes
Your daddy is by your side

If you should wake tomorrow and the fences are all torn down
The woods are full of howling beasts and there ain't nobody around
And everything seems foreign to your little ways
That's just the gods above making it safe to graze
The fox has its home, the bird has its nest
But the son of man has no place to lay his head and rest

No More Shall We Part
(2001)

As I Sat Sadly by Her Side
And No More Shall We Part
Hallelujah
Love Letter
Fifteen Feet of Pure White Snow
God is in the House
O My Lord
Sweetheart Come
We Came along this Road
The Sorrowful Wife
Gates to the Garden
Darker With the Day

Little Janey's Gone
A Grief Came Riding
A Good, Good Day
Bless His Ever-Loving Heart

As I Sat Sadly by Her Side

As I sat sadly by her side
At the window, through the glass
She stroked a kitten in her lap
And we watched the world as it fell past
Softly she spoke these words to me
And with brand-new eyes, open wide
We pressed our faces to the glass
As I sat sadly by her side

She said, 'Father, mother, sister, brother
Uncle, aunt, nephew, niece
Soldier, sailor, physician, labourer
Actor, scientist, mechanic, priest
Earth and moon and sun and stars
Planets and comets with tails blazing
All are there forever falling
Falling lovely and amazing'

Then she smiled and turned to me
And waited for me to reply
Her hair was falling down her shoulders
As I sat sadly by her side

As I sat sadly by her side
The kitten she did gently pass
Over to me and again we pressed
Our different faces to the glass
'That may be very well,' I said
'But watch that one falling in the street
See him gesture to his neighbours
See him trampled beneath their feet

All outward motion connects to nothing
For each is concerned with their immediate need
Witness the man reaching up from the gutter
See the other one stumbling on who does not see'

With trembling hand I turned toward her
And pushed the hair out of her eyes
The kitten jumped back to her lap
As I say sadly by her side

Then she drew the curtains down
And said, 'When will you ever learn
That what happens there beyond the glass
Is simply none of your concern?
God has given you but one heart
You are not a home for the hearts of your brothers
And God does not care for your benevolence
Any more than he cares for the lack of it in others
Nor does he care for those who sit
At windows in judgement of the world He created
While sorrows pile up around him
Ugly, useless and over-inflated'

At which she turned her head away
Great tears leaping from her eyes
I could not wipe the smile from my face
As I sat sadly by her side

And No More Shall We Part

And no more shall we part
It will no longer be necessary
No more will I say, dear heart
I am alone and she has left me

And no more shall we part
The contracts are drawn up, the ring is locked upon the finger
Never again will my letters start
Sadly, or in the depths of winter

And no more shall we part
All the hatchets have been buried now
And the birds will sing to your beautiful heart
Upon the bough

And no more shall we part
Your chain of command has been silenced now
And all of those birds would have sung to your beautiful heart
Anyhow

Lord, stay by me
Don't go down
I will never be free
If I'm not free now

Lord, stay by me
Don't go down
I never was free
What are you talking about?
For no more shall we part
And no more shall we part

Hallelujah

On the first day of May I took to the road
I'd been staring out the window most of the morning
I'd watched the rain claw at the glass
And a viscous wind blew hard and fast
I should have taken that as a warning
As a warning As a warning
As a warning

I'd given my nurse the weekend off
My meals were ill prepared
My typewriter had turned mute as a tomb
And my piano crouched in the corner of my room
With all its teeth bared
All its teeth bared All its teeth bared
All its teeth bared

Hallelujah Hallelujah
Hallelujah Hallelujah

I left my house without my coat
Something my nurse would not have allowed
And I took the small roads out of town
I passed a cow, the cow was brown
And my pyjamas clung to me like a shroud
Like a shroud Like a shroud
Like a shroud

There rose before me a little house
With all hope and dreams kept within
And a woman's voice close to my ear
Said, 'Why don't you come in here?

You looked soaked to the skin'
Soaked to the skin Soaked to the skin
Soaked to the skin

Hallelujah Hallelujah
Hallelujah Hallelujah

I turned to the woman, the woman was young
I extended a hearty salutation
But I knew if my nurse had been there
She would never in a thousand years
Permit me to accept that invitation
Invitation That invitation
Invitation

Now, you might think it wise to risk it all
To throw caution to the reckless wind
But with her hot cocoa and medication
My nurse had been my one salvation
So I turned back home
I turned back home I turned back home
Singing my song

Hallelujah
The tears are welling in my eyes again
Hallelujah
I need twenty big buckets to catch them in
Hallelujah
And twenty pretty girls to carry them down
Hallelujah
And twenty deep holes to bury them in
Hallelujah
The tears are welling in my eyes again

Hallelujah
I need twenty big buckets to catch them in
Hallelujah
And twenty pretty girls to carry them down
Hallelujah
And twenty deep holes to bury them in

Love Letter

I hold this letter in my hand
A plea, a petition, a kind of prayer
I hope it does as I have planned
Losing her again is more than I can bear
I kiss the cold, white envelope
I press my lips against her name
Two hundred words. We live in hope
The sky hangs heavy with rain

Love Letter Love Letter
Go get her Go get her
Love Letter Love Letter
Go tell her Go tell her

A wicked wind whips up the hill
A handful of hopeful words
I love her and I always will
The sky is ready to burst
Said something I did not mean to say
Said something I did not mean to say
Said something I did not mean to say
It all came out the wrong way

Love Letter Love Letter
Go get her Go get her
Love Letter Love Letter
Go tell her Go tell her

Rain your kisses down upon me
Rain your kisses down in storms
And for all who'll come before me
In your slowly fading forms

I'm going out of my mind
Will leave me standing in
The rain with a letter and a prayer
Whispered on the wind

Come back to me
Come back to me
O baby please come back to me

Fifteen Feet of Pure White Snow

Where is Mona?
She's long gone
Where is Mary?
She's taken her along
But they haven't put their mittens on
And there's fifteen feet of pure white snow

Where is Michael?
Where is Mark?
Where is Matthew
Now it's getting dark?
Where is John? They are all out back
Under fifteen feet of pure white snow

Would you please put down that telephone
We are under fifteen feet of pure white snow

I waved to my neighbour
My neighbour waved to me
But neighbour
Is my enemy
I kept waving my arms
Till I could not see
Under fifteen feet of pure white snow

Is anybody
Out there please?
It's too quiet in here
And I'm beginning to freeze
I've got icicles hanging
From my knees
Under fifteen feet of pure white snow

Is there anybody here who doesn't know?
We're under fifteen feet of pure white snow

Raise your hands up to the sky
Raise your hands up to the sky
Raise your hands up to the sky
Is it any wonder?
O my Lord O my Lord
O my Lord O my Lord

Doctor, Doctor
I'm going mad
This is the worst day
I've ever had
I can't remember
Ever feeling this bad
Under fifteen feet of pure white snow

Where's my nurse
I need some healing
I've been paralysed
By a lack of feeling
I can't even find
Anything worth stealing
Under fifteen feet of pure white snow

Is there anyone else who feels this low?
Under fifteen feet of pure white snow

Raise your hands up to the sky
Raise your hands up to the sky
Raise your hands up to the sky
Is it any wonder?
O my Lord O my Lord
O my Lord O my Lord

Save Yourself! Help Yourself!
Save Yourself! Help Yourself!
Save Yourself! Help Yourself!
Save Yourself! Help Yourself!

God is in the House

We've laid the cables and the wires
We've split the wood and stoked the fires
We've lit our town so there is no
Place for crime to hide
Our little church is painted white
And in the safety of the night
We all go quiet as a mouse
For the word is out
God is in the house
God is in the house
God is in the house
No cause for worry now
God is in the house

Moral sneaks in the White House
Computer geeks in the school house
Drug freaks in the crack house
We don't have that stuff here
We have a tiny little Force
But we need them of course
For the kittens in the trees
And at night we are on our knees
As quiet as a mouse
For God is in the house
God is in the house
No one's left in doubt
God is in the house

Homos roaming the streets in packs
Queer-bashers with tyre-jacks
Lesbian counter-attacks
That stuff is for the big cities
Our town is very pretty
With a pretty little square
We have a woman for a mayor
Our policy is firm but fair
Now that God is in the house
God is in the house
Any day now He'll come out
God is in the house

Well-meaning little therapists
Goose-stepping twelve-stepping Teetotalitarianists
The tipsy, the reeling and the drop-down pissed
We got no time for that stuff here
Zero crime and no fear
We've bred all our kittens white
So you can see them in the night
And we're all down on our knees
As quiet as a mouse
Since the word got out
From the North down to the South
For no one's left in doubt
There's no fear about
If we all hold hands and very quietly shout
God is in the house

O My Lord

I thought I'd take a walk today
It's a mistake I sometimes make
My children lay asleep in bed
My wife lay wide awake
I kissed her softly on the brow
I tried not to make a sound
But with stony eyes she looked at me
And gently squeezed my hand
Call it a premonition; call it a crazy vision
Call it intuition, something learned from mother
But when she looked up at me, I could clearly see
The Sword of Damocles hanging directly above her
O Lord O my Lord
O Lord
How have I offended thee?
Wrap your tender arms round me
O Lord O Lord
O My Lord

They called at me through the fence
They were not making any sense
They claimed that I had lost the plot
Kept saying that I was not
The man I used to be
They held their babes aloft
Threw marshmallows at the Security
And said that I'd grown soft
Call it intuition, a creeping suspicion
Their words of derision meant they hardly knew me
For even I could see in the way they looked at me
The Spear of Destiny sticking right through me

Now I'm at the hairdresser's
People watch me as they move past
A guy wearing plastic antlers
Presses his bum against the glass
Now I'm down on my hands and knees
And it's so fucking hot!
Someone cries, 'What are you looking for?'
I scream, 'The plot, baby, the plot!'
I grab my telephone, call my wife at home
She screams, 'Leave us alone!' I say, 'Hey, it's only me'
The hairdresser with his scissors holds up the mirror
I look back and shiver; I can't even believe what I can see
O Lord O my Lord
O Lord
How have I offended thee?
Wrap your tender arms round me
O Lord O Lord
O My Lord

Be mindful of the prayers you send
Pray hard but pray with care
For the tears that you are crying now
Are just your answered prayers
The ladders of life that we scale merrily
Move mysteriously around
So that when you think you're climbing up
In fact you're climbing down
Into the hollows of glamour, where with spikes and hammer
With telescopic camera, they choose to turn the screw
O I hate them, Ma! O I hate them, Pa!
O I hate them all for what they went and did to you

O Lord O my Lord
O Lord
How have I offended thee?
Wrap your tender arms round me
O Lord O Lord
O My Lord

Sweetheart Come

Come over here, babe
It ain't that bad
I don't claim to understand
The troubles that you've had
But the dogs you say they fed you to
Lay their muzzles in your lap
And the lions that they led you to
Lie down and take a nap
The ones you fear are wind and air
And I love you without measure
It seems we can be happy now
Be it better late than never

Sweetheart, come
Sweetheart, come
Sweetheart, come
Sweetheart, come to me

The burdens that you carry now
Are not of your creation
So let's not weep for their evil deeds
But for their lack of imagination
Today's the time for courage, babe
Tomorrow can be for forgiving
And if he touches you again with his stupid hands
His life won't be worth living

Sweetheart, come
Sweetheart, come
Sweetheart, come
Sweetheart, come to me

Walk with me now under the stars
For it's a clear and easy pleasure
And be happy in my company
For I love you without measure
Walk with me now under the stars
It's a safe and easy pleasure
It seems we can be happy now
It's late but it ain't never
It's late but it ain't never
It's late but it ain't never

We Came along this Road

I left by the back door
With my wife's lover's smoking gun
I don't know what I was hoping for
I hit the road at a run
I was your lover
I was your man
There never was no other
I was your friend
Till we came along this road
Till we came along this road
Till we came along this road

I ain't sent you no letters, Ma
But I'm looking quite a trip
The world spinning beneath me, Ma
Guns blazing at my hip
You were my lover
You were my friend
There never was no other
On whom I could depend
Then we came along this road
We came along this road
We came along this road

The Sorrowful Wife

I married my wife on the day of the eclipse
Our friends awarded her courage with gifts
Now as the nights grow longer and the season shifts
I look to my sorrowful wife
Who is quietly tending her flowers
Who is quietly tending her . . .

The water is high on the beckoning river
I made her a promise I could not deliver
And the cry of the birds sends a terrible shiver
Through me and my sorrowful wife
Who is shifting the furniture around
Who is shifting the furniture around

Now we sit beneath the knotted Yew
And the bluebells bob up around our shoes
The task of remembering the telltale clues
Goes to my lovely, my sorrowful wife
Who is counting the days on her fingers
Who is counting the days on her . . .

Come on and help me babe
Come on now
Help me babe
I was blind
The grass here grows long and high
Twists right up to the sky
White clouds roll on by
Come on now and help me babe
I am a fool
I was blind, babe
Come on now

A loose wind last night blew down
Black trees bent to the ground
Their blossoms made such a sound
That I could not hear myself think babe
Come on now
And help me babe
Help me now
I was blind
I was a fool

Gates to the Garden

Past the ivy-covered windows of The Angel
Down Athenaeum Lane to the cathedral
Through the churchyard I wandered
Sat for a spell there and I pondered
My back to the gates of the garden

Fugitive fathers, sickly infants, decent mothers
Run-a-ways and suicidal lovers
Assorted boxes of ordinary bones
Of aborted plans and sudden shattered hopes
In unlucky rows, up to the gates of the garden

Won't you meet me at the gates
Won't you meet me at the gates
Won't you meet me at the gates
To the garden

Beneath the creeping shadow of the tower
The bell from St Edmunds informs me of the hour
I turn to find you waiting there for me
In sunlight and I see the way you breathe
Alive and leaning on the gates of the garden

Leave these ancient places to the angels
Let the saints attend to the keeping of their cathedrals
And leave the dead beneath the ground so cold
For God is in this hand that I hold
As we open up the gates of the garden

Won't you meet me at the gates
Won't you meet me at the gates
Won't you meet me at the gates
To the garden

Darker With the Day

As so with that, I thought I'd take a final walk
The tide of public opinion had started to abate
The neighbours, bless them, had turned out to be all talk
I could see their frightened faces peering at me through the gate

I was looking for an end to this, for some kind of closure
Time moved so rapidly, I had no hope of keeping track of it
I thought of my friends who had died of exposure
And I remembered other ones who had died from the lack of it

And in my best shoes I started falling forward down the street
I stopped at a church and jostled through the crowd
And love followed just behind me, panting at my feet
As the steeple tore the stomach from a lonely little cloud

Inside I sat, seeking the presence of a God
I searched through the pictures in a leather-bound book
I found a woolly lamb dosing in an issue of blood
And a gilled Jesus shivering on a fisherman's hook

Babe
It seems so long
Since you've been gone away
And I
Just got to say
That it grows darker with the day

Back on the street I saw a great big smiling sun
It was a Good day and an Evil day and all was bright and new
And it seemed to me that most destruction was being done
By those who could not choose between the two

Amateurs, dilettantes, hacks, cowboys, clones
The streets groan with little Caesars, Napoleons and cunts
With their building blocks and tiny plastic phones
Counting on their fingers, with crumbs down their fronts

I passed by your garden, saw you with your flowers
The Magnolias, Camellias and Azaleas so sweet
And I stood there invisible in the panicking crowds
You looked so beautiful in the rising heat

I smell smoke, see little fires bursting on the lawns
People carry on regardless, listening to their hands
Great cracks appear in the pavement, the earth yawns
Bored and disgusted, to do us down

Babe
It seems so long
Since you've been gone away
And I
Just got to say
That it grows darker with the day

These streets are frozen now. I come and go
Full of a longing for something I do not know
My father sits slumped in the deepening snow
As I search, in and out, above, about, below

Babe
It's been so long
Since you've been gone away
And I
Just got to say
That it grows darker with the day

Little Janey's Gone

Janey's gone now and she won't be back no more
It was only yesterday I went knocking on her door
And now she's gone away
We won't see her no more
Little Janey's gone now Janey's gone now
Janey's gone now Janey's gone
Little Janey's gone now Janey's gone now
Janey's gone away
O yes she's gone away
O man, that's for sure
Little Janey's gone now Janey's gone now
Janey's gone away

Janey's gone. O people! O Lord! Little Janey's gone
She was the only one that we all could depend on
And now she's gone away
We won't see her round no more
Little Janey's gone now Janey's gone now
Janey's gone now Janey's gone
Little Janey's gone now Janey's gone now
Janey's gone away
Yes she's gone away
O yeah! That's for sure
Little Janey's gone now Janey's gone now
Janey's gone away

Janey's gone now and she won't be back no more
We'll have to find some other place to go and score
'Cause now she's gone, don't you see
They're gunna throw away the key

Little Janey's gone down Janey's gone down
Janey's gone down Janey's gone
Little Janey's gone down Janey's gone down
Janey's gone away

A Grief Came Riding

A grief came riding on the wind
Up the sullen River Thames
I was sitting on the bank with my mouth open
And I felt it enter in
I began thinking about our wedding day
And how love was a vow
I was thinking about the chamber door
That only we can enter now
I was thinking about our ancient friends
And of kissing them goodbye
Then the wind blew under Battersea Bridge
And a tear broke from my eye
And I got thinking about London
How nothing good ever came from this town
And if the Thames wasn't so filthy
I'd jump in the river and drown
Don't be afraid, babe, come on down
I'm just sitting here thinking aloud

A grief came riding down the wind
Up the river where the bridges crouch
Blowing people back and forth
From the marital bed to the psychiatric couch
Blowing people far apart
Blowing others so they collide
Blowing some poor bastard right out of the water
Blowing another one over the side
Hear the ancient iron bridge
Listen to it groan
With the weight of a thousand people
Leaving or returning home
To their failures, to their boredoms

To their husbands and their wives
Who are carving them up for dinner
Before they even arrive
Don't be afraid, come on down
I'm just sitting here thinking aloud

Now look there just below the water
See the Saviour of the human race
With the fishes and the frogs
Has found his final resting place
Don't be afraid, come on down
I'm just sitting here thinking aloud

A Good, Good Day

See the little cloud up in the sky
It's a good, good day today
See the little cloud pass on by
It's a good, good day today
Mary comes now, let Mary be
Can you see her down on the street?
Mary's laughing, 'cause Mary sees
That she's wearing that dress for me
There can be times
When all things
Come together
And for a moment
Under a clear sky
You can believe
You hold your breath
For this moment
But do not breathe
This day, I know
Is a good day
I know
It's a good day
I know
Today

Hear her feet skipping up the stairs
It's a good, good day today
She is the answer to all of my prayers
It's a good, good day today
Mary comes now, she don't knock
She's running on her own little clock
Mary's laughing, 'cause Mary knows
That this day was made for us

And any fool knows . . . yeah
And any fool sees
That the future . . . yeah
Is down on its knees
Let 'em cry, let 'em weep
Let the tears roll down their cheeks
'Cause I can believe
In the one that is standing in front of me
On this day, which I know
Is a good day, yeah I know
Is a good day, I know
Today

See her breasts, how they rise and fall
It's a good, good day today
And she knows I've used that line before
It's a good, good day today
Mary's laughing, she don't mind
'Cause she knows she's one of a kind
Mary's happy just to be
Standing next to me
And any fool knows . . . yeah
That the wind always blows
Something to someone . . . yeah
Once in a while
So let it rain
Let it pour
Let the wind howl through your door
'Cause right now for this moment
I will for ever be standing next to her
On this good day, yeah
It's a good day, yeah I know
It's a good day, I've told you so
Today

Bless His Ever-Loving Heart

Bless His ever-loving heart
Only He knows who you are
He may seem so very far
But bless His ever-loving heart

And when you're feeling sad
And everywhere you look
You can't believe the things you see
And when it's all come down so hard
And beauty lies exhausted in the street

Hold His ever-loving hand
Even when you do not understand
Sorrow has its natural end
Hold His ever-loving hand

And when you're feeling low
And everyone you meet
You can't believe the things they say
And when there is no place left to go
Where someone isn't moving you
A little further down the way

Bless His ever-loving heart
What you do is what you are
When it's all come down so hard
Bless His ever-loving heart

Hold His ever-loving hand
When it seems you haven't got a friend
Only He knows who you are
Bless His ever-loving heart

Nocturama
(2003)

Wonderful Life
He Wants You
Right Out of Your Hand
Bring It On
Dead Man in My Bed
Still in Love
There is a Town
Rock of Gibraltar
She Passed By My Window
Babe, I'm on Fire

Shoot Me Down
Swing Low
Everything Must Converge

Wonderful Life

Come in, babe
Across these purple fields
The sun has sunk behind you
Across these purple fields
That idiot-boy in the corner
Is speaking deviated truths
Come on, admit it, babe
It's a wonderful life
If you can find it
If you can find it
If you can find it
It's a wonderful life that you bring
Ooh, it's a wonderful thing

Speak our secret into your hands
And hold it in between
Plunge your hands into the water
And drown it in the sea
There will be nothing between us, baby
But the air that we breathe
Don't cry
It's a wonderful, wonderful life
If you can find it
If you can find it
If you can find it
It's a wonderful life that you bring
It's a wonderful, wonderful thing

We can build our dungeons in the air
And sit and cry the blues
We can stomp across this world
With nails hammered through our shoes

We can join that troubled chorus
Who criticize and accuse
It don't matter much
We got nothing much to lose
But this wonderful life
If you can find it
And when you find it
And when you find it
It's a wonderful life that you bring
It's a wonderful, wonderful, wonderful thing

Sometimes our secrets are all we've got
With our lives we must defend
Sometimes the air between us, babe
Is unbearably thin
Sometimes it's wise to lay down your gloves
And just give in
Come in, come in
Come in, come in
To this wonderful life
If you can find it
And if you find it
It's a wonderful life that you bring
It's a wonderful, wonderful thing
It's a wonderful life
It's a wonderful life

He Wants You

In his boat and through the dark he rowed
Chained to oar and the night and the wind that blowed
Horribly round his ears
Under the bridge and into your dreams he soars
While you lie alone in that idea-free sleep of yours
That you've been sleeping now for years

And he wants you
He wants you
He is straight and he is true
Ooh hoo hoo

Beneath the hanging cliffs and under the many stars where
He will move, all amongst your tangled hair
And deep into the sea
And you will wake and walk and draw the blind
And feel some presence there behind
And turn to see what that may be
Oh, babe, it's me

And he wants you
He wants you
He is straight and he is true
Ooh hoo hoo

Right Out of Your Hand

Please forgive me
If I appear unkind
But any fool can tell you
It's all in your mind

Down in the meadow
The old lion stirs
Puts his hand 'cross his mouth
He has no use for words

Poor little girl
With your handful of snow
Poor little girl
Had no way to know

And you've got me eating
You've got me eating
You've got me eating
Right out of your hand

I mean you no harm
When I tell you you're blind
Give a sucker an even break
He'll lose it all, every time

The airborne starlings circle
Over the frozen fields
The hollyhocks hang harmlessly
And the old lion yields

And you've got me eating
You've got me eating
You've got me eating
Right out of your hand

Bring It On

This garden that I built for you
That you sit in now and yearn
I will never leave it, dear
I could not bear to return
And find it all untended
With the trees all bended low
This garden is our home, dear
And I got nowhere else to go

So bring it on
Bring it on
Every little tear
Bring it on
Every useless fear
Bring it on
All your shattered dreams
And I'll scatter them into the sea
Into the sea

The geraniums on your window sill
The carnations, dear, and the daffodil
Well, they're ordinary flowers
But they long for the light of your touch
And of your trembling will
Ah, you're trembling still
And I am trembling too
To be perfectly honest I don't know
Quite what else to do

So bring it on
Bring it on
Every neglected dream
Bring it on
Every little scheme
Bring it on
Every little fear
And I'll make them disappear

So bring it on, bring it on
Bring it on
Every little thing
Bring it on
Every tiny fear
Bring it on
Every shattered dream
And I'll scatter them into the sea

Dead Man in My Bed

She sat in a wicker chair, her eyes they were downcast
She breathed in the future, by breathing out the past
The die is done, the die is shook, the die is duly cast
There is a dead man in my bed, she said
That smile you see upon his face
It's been there for many days
There's a dead man in my bed

I ain't been feeling that good too much no more, she said, I
swear
She pointed at the bedroom door and said I ain't going in
there
She leaped out of her seat and screamed someone's not
concentrating here
There is a dead man in my bed, she said
I ain't speaking metaphorically
His eyes are open but he cannot see
There's a dead man in my bed

The leaves outside the window waved, all brown, they were,
and falling
Even I could tell the atmosphere in here was utterly appalling
The phone it rang incessantly but nobody was calling
There's a dead man in my bed, she said
And though he keeps on taking notes
I swear this ain't some kind of hoax
Dead man in my bed

Now she's in the kitchen, rattling those pots and pans
I'd cook him something nice, she said, but he refuses to wash
his hands
He used to be so good to me, now he smells so fucking bad
There is a dead man in my bed, she said
I keep poking at him with my stick
But his skin is just so fucking thick
There's a dead man in my bed

We've gotta get it all together
We've gotta get it all together
We've gotta get it all together
We've gotta get it all together

Still in Love

The cops are hanging around the house
The cars outside look like they've got the blues
The moon don't know if it's day or night
Everybody's creeping around with plastic covers on their
shoes
You're making coffee for everyone concerned
Someone points to this and someone points to that
Everyone is saying that you should lie down
But you ain't having none of that
And I say to the sleepy summer rain
With a complete absence of pain
You might think I'm crazy
But I'm still in love with you

Hide your eyes, hide your tears
Hide your face, my love
Hide your ribbons, hide your bows
Hide your coloured cotton gloves
Hide your trinkets, hide your treasures
Hide your neatly scissored locks
Hide your memories, hide them all
Stuff them in a cardboard box
Or throw them into the street below
Leave them to the wind and the rain and the snow
For you might think I'm crazy
But I'm still in love with you

Call me up, baby, and I will answer your call
Call me up but remember I am no use to you at all

Now, you're standing at the top of the stairs
One hand on the banister, a flower in your hair
The other one resting on your hip
Without a solitary care
I fall to sleep in the summer rain
With no single memory of pain
And you might think I'm crazy
But I'm still in love with you

There is a Town

There is a town
Where I was born
Far far away
Across the sea

And in that town
Where I was born
I would dream
That one day
I would leave
And cross the sea

And so it goes
And so it seems
That God lives only in our dreams
In our dreams

And now I live
In this town
I walk these dark streets
Up and down, up and down
Under a dark sky
And I dream
That one day
I'll go back home

And so it goes
And so it seems
That God lives only in our dreams
In our dreams

Rock of Gibraltar

Let me say this to you
I'll be steadfast and true
And my love will never falter

The sea would crash about us
The waves would lash about us
I'll be your Rock of Gibraltar

Sometimes it's hard
And we're both caught off guard
But there's nothing I would ever alter

The wind could howl round our ears
For the next thousand years
I'd still be your Rock of Gibraltar

The best thing I done
Was to make you the one
Who I'd walk with down to the altar

You'd stand by me
And together we'd be
That great, steady Rock of Gibraltar

Under the big yellow moon
On our honeymoon
I took you on a trip to Malta

And all through the night
You held me so tight
Your great, steady Rock of Gibraltar

Could the powers that be
Ever foresee
That things could so utterly alter?

All the plans that we laid
Could soon be betrayed
Betrayed like the Rock of Gibraltar

She Passed By My Window

She passed by my window
Her eyes were all aglow
And bent to pick her glove she'd dropped
From the bright and brittle snow

Nature had spoken it in the Spring
With apple, plum and brand new pear
Have you time for my company?
No, I said, I have none to spare

You gotta sanctify my love
You gotta sanctify my love
You gotta sanctify my love
I ain't no lover-boy

For apple, plum and brand new pear
Soon wither on the ground
She slapped the snow from off her glove
And moved on without a sound

You gotta sanctify my love
You gotta sanctify my love
You gotta sanctify my love
I ain't no lover-boy

Babe, I'm on Fire

Father says it, Mother says it
Sister says it, Brother says it
Uncle says it, Auntie says it
Everyone at the party says
Babe, I'm on fire
Babe, I'm on fire

The horse says it, the pig says it
The judge in his wig says it
The fox and the rabbit
And the nun in her habit says
Babe, I'm on fire
Babe, I'm on fire

My mate Bill Gates says it
The President of the United States says it
The slacker and the worker
The girl in her burqa says
Babe, I'm on fire
Babe, I'm on fire

The general with his tank says it
The man at the bank says it
The soldier with his rocket
And the mouse in my pocket says
Babe, I'm on fire
Babe, I'm on fire

The drug-addled wreck
With a needle in his neck says it
The drunk says it, punk says it
The brave Buddhist monk says

Babe, I'm on fire
Babe, I'm on fire

Hit me up, baby, and knock me down
Drop what you're doing and come around
We can hold hands till the sun goes down
'Cause I know
That you
And I
Can be
Together
'Cause I love you

The blind referee says it
The unlucky amputee says it
The giant killer bee
Landing on my knee says
Babe, I'm on fire
Babe, I'm on fire

The cop with his breathalyzer
The paddy with his fertilizer
The man in the basement
That's getting a taste for it says
Babe, I'm on fire
Babe, I'm on fire

The fucked-up Rastafarian says it
The dribbling libertarian says it
The sweet little goth
With the ears of cloth says
Babe, I'm on fire
Babe, I'm on fire

The cross-over country singer says it
The hump-backed bell ringer says it
The swinger, the flinger
The outraged right-winger says
Babe, I'm on fire
Babe, I'm on fire

The man going hiking says it
The misunderstood Viking says it
The man at the rodeo
And the lonely old Eskimo says
Babe, I'm on fire
Babe, I'm on fire

Hit me up, baby, and knock me down
Drop what you're doing and come around
We can hold hands till the sun goes down
'Cause I know
That you
And I
Can be
Together
'Cause I love you

The mild little Christian says it
The wild Sonny Liston says it
The pimp and the gimp
And the guy with the limp says
Babe, I'm on fire
Babe, I'm on fire

The blind piano tuner says it
The Las Vegas crooner says it
The hooligan mooner
Holding a schooner says

Babe, I'm on fire
Babe, I'm on fire

The Chinese contortionist says it
The backyard abortionist says it
The poor Pakistani
With his lamb biriani says
Babe, I'm on fire
Babe, I'm on fire

The hopeless defendant says it
The toilet attendant says it
The pornographer, the stenographer
The fashion photographer says
Babe, I'm on fire
Babe, I'm on fire

The college professor says it
The vicious cross-dresser says it
Grandma and Grandpa
In the back of the car says
Babe, I'm on fire
Babe, I'm on fire

Hit me up, baby, and knock me down
Drop what you're doing and come around
We can hold hands till the sun goes down
'Cause I know
That you
And I
Can be
Together
'Cause I love you

The hack at the doorstep says it
The midwife with her forceps says it
The demented young lady
Who is roasting her baby
On the fire
Babe, I'm on fire

The athlete with his hernia says it
Picasso with his *Guernica* says it
My wife with her furniture
Everybody!
Babe, I'm on fire
Babe, I'm on fire

The laughing hyena says it
The homesick Polish cleaner says it
The man from the Klan
With a torch in his hand says
Babe, I'm on fire
Babe, I'm on fire

The Chinese herbologist says it
The Christian apologist says it
The dog and the frog
Sitting on a log says
Babe, I'm on fire
Babe, I'm on fire

The fox-hunting toff says it
The horrible moth says it
The doomed homosexual
With the persistent cough says
Babe, I'm on fire
Babe, I'm on fire

Hit me up, baby, and knock me down
Drop what you're doing and come around
We can hold hands till the sun goes down
'Cause I know
That you
And I
Can be
Together
'Cause I love you

The Papist with his soul says it
The rapist on a roll says it
Jack says it, Jill says it
As they roll down the hill
Babe, I'm on fire
Babe, I'm on fire

The clever circus flea says it
The sailor on the sea says it
The man from the *Daily Mail*
With his dead refugee says
Babe, I'm on fire
Babe, I'm on fire

The hymen-busting Zulu says it
The proud kangaroo says it
The koala, the echidna
And the platypus too says
Babe, I'm on fire
Babe, I'm on fire

The disgraced country vicar says it
The crazed guitar picker says it
The beatnik, the peacenik
The apparatchik says

Babe, I'm on fire
Babe, I'm on fire

The deranged midnight stalker says it
García Lorca says it
The hit man, Walt Whitman
And the halitotic talker says
Babe, I'm on fire
Babe, I'm on fire

Hit me up, baby, and knock me down
Drop what you're doing and come around
We can hold hands till the sun goes down
'Cause I know
That you
And I
Can be
Together
'Cause I love you

The wine taster with his nose says it
The fireman with his hose says it
The pedestrian, the equestrian
The tap-dancer with his toes says
Babe, I'm on fire
Babe, I'm on fire

The beast in the beauty pageant
The pimply real estate agent
The beach-comber, the roamer
The girl in a coma says
Babe, I'm on fire
Babe, I'm on fire

The old rock 'n' roller
With his two-seater stroller
And the fan in the van
With the abominable plan says
Babe, I'm on fire
Babe, I'm on fire

The menstruating Jewess says it
The nervous stewardess says it
The hijacker, the backpacker
The cunning safe-cracker says
Babe, I'm on fire
Babe, I'm on fire

The sports commentator says it
The old alligator says it
The tennis pro with his racket
The loon in the straitjacket
Babe, I'm on fire
Babe, I'm on fire

Hit me up, baby, and knock me down
Drop what you're doing and come around
We can hold hands till the sun goes down
'Cause I know
That you
And I
Can be
Together
'Cause I love you

The butcher with his cleaver says it
The mad basket weaver says it
The jaded boxing writer

And the glass-jawed fighter says
Babe, I'm on fire
Babe, I'm on fire

The old town crier says it
The inveterate liar says it
The pilchard, the bream
And the trout in the stream
Babe, I'm on fire
Babe, I'm on fire

The war correspondent says it
The enthused and the despondent says it
The electrician, the mortician
And the man going fishin' says
Babe, I'm on fire
Babe, I'm on fire

The cattleman from Down Under says it
The patriot with his plunder says it
Watching a boat full of refugees
Sinking into the sea
Babe, I'm on fire
Babe, I'm on fire

The silicone junky says it
The corporate flunky says it
The Italian designer
With his rickshaw in China says
Babe, I'm on fire
Babe, I'm on fire

Hit me up, baby, and knock me down
Drop what you're doing and come around
We can hold hands till the sun goes down
'Cause I know
That you
And I
Can be
Together
'Cause I love you

The trucker with his juggernaut says it
The lost astronaut says it
The share cropper, the bent copper
The compulsive shopper says
Babe, I'm on fire
Babe, I'm on fire

The Viennese vampire says it
The cowboy round his campfire says it
The game show panellist
The Jungian analyst says
Babe, I'm on fire
Babe, I'm on fire

Warren says it, Blixa says it
The lighting guy and mixer says it
Mick says it, Marty says it
Everyone at the party says
Babe, I'm on fire
Babe, I'm on fire

Hit me up, baby, and knock me down
Drop what you're doing and come around
We can hold hands till the sun goes down
'Cause I know
That you
And I
Can be
Together
'Cause I love you

Shoot Me Down

On those sentimental nights
You hold me in your sights
And shoot me down

And though there ain't no enemy here
You keep me very near
And shoot me down
Shoot me down

Your hands, they flutter up
Armed and dangerous, my buttercup
And shoot me down
In flames

Stand back, baby, stand back and let me breathe
I think I'm falling out of here
I can hear the grass grow, I can hear the melting snow
I can feel your breath against my ear
I might just disappear
Wouldn't that be nice
Wouldn't that be nice
Well, wouldn't that be nice

I look into your eyes
And it comes as no great surprise
You're gonna shoot me down
Shoot me down

I know that when you smile
It'll only be just a short, little while
Shoot me down
In flames

Shoot me down
In flames
Shoot me down
In flames

Swing Low

How is little Thomas Magee?
Thomas Magee, he swallowed a key
Did he die, little Thomas Magee?
Hardly . . . hardly . . . just let him be
He's wiser now, little Thomas Magee

I called this cat on the telephone
My heart was beating in my chest
I'd eaten something I could not digest
But the phone kept ringing, there's no one home

I ran to his house, rapped on the window
My blood was pumping much too fast
As I stuck my fingers through the glass
I heard strange music playing on the radio

Swing low
Swing low
Swing low
Swing low
Way down low
And carry me home

Pray like Peter, preach like Paul
Jesus died to save us all
I climbed through the window, I crawled on the floor
I ripped apart the furniture
But I still couldn't find what I was looking for

The problems, dear, we claim as our own
Cannot be solved, they must be outgrown
The bottomless knowledge that cannot be known
And the empty ringing of the telephone
And the strange music playing on the radio

Swing low
Swing low
Swing low
Swing low
Way down low
And carry me home

Where did you go?
Where did you go?
Swing low, baby, save my soul
Where did you go?
Where did you go?
Swing low, baby, save my soul

Swing low
Swing low
Swing low
And carry me home

Everything Must Converge

Everything must converge
In time
And so it goes
By and by

Everything must converge
Some day
Some how
Some way

Everything must converge
In time
So it seems
By and by

Every little thing must converge
It's true
By and by
So they say

Like the river that runs to the sea
Like the sun going down on me

Everything must converge
One day
I hope
I pray

Everything must converge
It's true
In time
Me and you

Like the river that runs to the sea
Like the sun going down on me

Everything must converge
Everything must converge
Everything must converge

Abatttoir Blues/The Lyre of Orpheus (2004)

Get Ready for Love
Cannibal's Hymn
Hiding All Away
Messiah Ward
There She Goes, My Beautiful World
Nature Boy
Abattoir Blues
Let the Bells Ring
Fable of the Brown Ape
The Lyre of Orpheus
Breathless
Babe, You Turn Me On
Easy Money
Supernaturally
Spell
Carry Me
O Children

She's Leaving You
Under This Moon

Get Ready for Love

Get ready for love! Praise Him!
Get ready for love! Praise Him!
Get ready for love! Get ready!

Well, most of all nothing much ever really happens
And God rides high up in the ordinary sky
Until we find ourselves at our most distracted
And the miracle that was promised creeps quietly by

Calling every boy and girl
Calling all around the world
Calling every boy and girl
Calling all around the world

Get ready for love! Praise Him!
Get ready for love! Praise Him!

The mighty wave their hankies from their high-windowed
  palace
Sending grief and joy down in supportable doses
And we search high and low without mercy or malice
While the gate to the Kingdom swings shut and closes

Calling every boy and girl
Calling all around the world
Calling every boy and girl
Calling all around the world

Praise Him till you've forgotten what you're praising Him for
Praise Him till you've forgotten what you're praising Him for
Then praise Him a little bit more

Yeah, praise Him a little bit more
Praise Him till you've forgotten what you're praising Him for
Praise Him till you've forgotten what you're praising Him for
Praise Him a little bit more
Yeah, praise Him a little bit more

Get ready for love! Praise Him!
Get ready for love! Get ready!

I searched the Seven Seas and I've looked under the carpet
And browsed through the brochures that govern the skies
Then I was just hanging around, doing nothing and looked
  up to see
His face burned in the retina of your eyes

Calling every boy and girl
Calling all around the world
Calling every boy and girl
Calling all around the world

Get ready for love! Praise Him!
Get ready for love! Praise Him!

Cannibal's Hymn

You have a heart and I have a key
Lie back and let me unlock you
Those heathens you hang with down by the sea
All they want to do is defrock you
I know a river where we can dream
It will swell up, burst its banks, babe, and rock you
But if you're gonna dine with them cannibals
Sooner or later, darling, you're gonna get eaten
But I'm glad you've come around here with your animals
And your heart that is bruised but unbeaten
And beating like a drum

I will sit like a bird on a fence
Sing you songs with a happy ending
Swoop down and tell you that it don't make sense
To attack the very thing you're defending
Didn't I just buy that dress for you?
That pink paper pinafore that you keep mending
Well, if you're gonna dine with the cannibals
Sooner or later, darling, you're gonna get eaten
But I'm glad you've come around here with your animals
And your heart that is banging and bleating
And banging like a gong

I can see that they've hurt you, dear
Here is some moonlight to cloak us
And I will never desert you here
Unpetalled among the crocus
Allow me, my love, to allay your fear
As I swim, in and out of focus
But if you're gonna dine with the cannibals
Sooner or later, darling, you're gonna get eaten

But I'm glad you've come around here with your animals
And your heart that is bruised but bleating
And bleeding like a lamb
Banging like a gong
Beating like a drum

Hiding All Away

You went looking for me, dear
Down by the sea
You found some little silver fish
But you didn't find me
I was hiding, dear, hiding all away
I was hiding, dear, hiding all away

You went to the museum
You climbed a spiral stair
You searched for me all among
The knowledgeable air
I was hidden, babe, hiding all away
I was hiding, dear, hiding all away

You entered the cathedral
When you heard the solemn knell
I was not sitting with the gargoyles
I was not swinging from the bell
I was hiding, dear, I was hiding all away
I was hiding, dear, hiding all away

You asked an electrician
If he'd seen me round his place
He touched you with his fingers
Sent sparks zapping out your face
I was hidden, dear, hiding all away
I was not there, dear, hiding all away

You went and asked your doctor
To get some advice
He shot you full of pethidine
And then he billed you twice

But I was hiding, dear, hiding all away
But I was hiding, dear, hiding all away

You approached a high court judge
You thought he'd be on the level
He wrapped a rag around your face
And beat you with his gavel
I was hiding, babe, hiding all away
I was hidden, dear, hiding all away

You asked at the local constabulary
They said, he's up to his same old tricks
They leered at you with their baby blues
And rubbed jelly on their sticks
I had to get out of there, babe, hiding all away
I had to get out of there, dear, hiding all away

You searched through all my poets
From Sappho through to Auden
I saw the book fall from your hands
As you slowly died of boredom
I had been there, dear, but I was not there anymore
I had been there, now I'm hiding all away

You walked into the hall of fame
And approached my imitators
Some were stuffing their faces with caviar
Some were eating cold potatoes
I was hiding, dear, hiding all away
I was hiding, dear, hiding all away

You asked a famous cook if he'd seen me
He opened his oven wide
He basted you with butter, babe
And made you crawl inside

I was not in there, dear, hiding all away
I was not in there, dear, hiding all away

You asked the butcher
Who lifted up his cleaver
Stuck his fist up your dress
Said he must've been mad to leave you
But I had to get away, dear hiding all away
I had to get away, dear, I was hidden all away

Some of us, we hide away
Some of us, we don't
Some will live to love another day
And some of us won't
But we all know there is a law
And that law, it is love
And we all know there's a war coming
Coming from above

There is a war coming
There is a war coming

Messiah Ward

I hope you're sitting comfortably
I saved you the best seat in the house
Right up in the front row
The stars have been torn down
The moon is locked away
And the land is banked in frozen snow

You are a force of nature, dear
Your breath curls from your lips
As the trees bend down their branches
And touch you with their fingertips
They're bringing out the dead, now
It's easy just to look away
They are bringing out the dead, now
It's been a strange, strange day

We could navigate our position by the stars
But they've taken out the stars
The stars have all gone
I'm glad you've come along
We could comprehend our condition by the moon
But they've ordered the moon not to shine
Still, I'm glad you've come along
I was worried out of my mind
'Cause they keep bringing out the dead
It's easy just to look away
They're bringing out the dead, now
And it's been a long, strange day

You can move up a little closer
I will throw a blanket over
We can weigh all the tears in one hand

Against the laughter in the other
We could be hanging around here for centuries
Trying to make sense of this, my dear
While the planets try to get organized
Way above the stratosphere
But they keep bringing out the dead, now
It's easy if we just walk away
They keep bringing out the dead, now
It's been a long, long day

Look away
Look away

There She Goes, My Beautiful World

The wintergreen, the juniper
The cornflower and the chicory
All the words you said to me
Still vibrating in the air
The elm, the ash and the linden tree
The dark and deep, enchanted sea
The trembling moon and the stars unfurled
There she goes, my beautiful world

There she goes, my beautiful world
There she goes, my beautiful world
There she goes, my beautiful world
There she goes again

John Wilmot penned his poetry riddled with the pox
Nabukov wrote on index cards, at a lectern, in his socks
St John of the Cross did his best stuff imprisoned in a box
And Johnny Thunders was half alive when he wrote 'Chinese
  Rocks'

Well, me, I'm lying here, with nothing in my ears
Me, I'm lying here, with nothing in my ears
Me, I'm lying here, for what seems years
I'm just lying on my bed with nothing in my head

Send that stuff on down to me
Send that stuff on down to me
Send that stuff on down to me
Send that stuff on down to me

There she goes, my beautiful world
There she goes, my beautiful world

There she goes, my beautiful world
There she goes again

Karl Marx squeezed his carbuncles while writing *Das Kapital*
And Gaugin, he buggered off, man, and went all tropical
While Philip Larkin stuck it out in a library in Hull
And Dylan Thomas died drunk in St Vincent's hospital

I will kneel at your feet
I will lie at your door
I will rock you to sleep
I will roll on the floor
And I'll ask for nothing
Nothing in this life
I'll ask for nothing
Give me everlasting life

I just want to move the world
I just want to move the world
I just want to move the world
I just want to move

There she goes, my beautiful world
There she goes, my beautiful world
There she goes, my beautiful world
There she goes again

So if you got a trumpet, get on your feet, brother, and blow it
If you've got a field that don't yield, well, get up and hoe it
I look at you and you look at me and deep in our hearts
  know it
That you weren't much of a muse, but then I weren't much
  of a poet

I will be your slave
I will peel you grapes
Up on your pedestal
With your ivory and apes
With your book of ideas
With your alchemy
O come on
Send that stuff on down to me

Send that stuff on down to me
Send that stuff on down to me
Send that stuff on down to me
Send that stuff on down to me
Send it all around the world
'Cause here she comes, my beautiful girl

There she goes, my beautiful world
There she goes, my beautiful world
There she goes, my beautiful world
There she goes again

Nature Boy

I was just a boy when I sat down
To watch the news on TV
I saw some ordinary slaughter
I saw some routine atrocity
My father said, don't look away
You got to be strong, you got to be bold, now
He said that in the end it is beauty
That is going to save the world, now

And she moves among the sparrows
And she floats upon the breeze
She moves among the flowers
She moves something deep inside of me

I was walking around the flower show like a leper
Coming down with some kind of nervous hysteria
When I saw you standing there, green eyes, black hair
Up against the pink and purple wisteria
You said, hey, nature boy, are you looking at me
With some unrighteous intention?
My knees went weak, I couldn't speak, I was having thoughts
That were not in my best interests to mention

And she moves among the flowers
And she floats upon the smoke
She moves among the shadows
She moves me with just one little look

You took me back to your place
And dressed me up in a deep-sea diver's suit
You played the patriot, you raised the flag
And I stood at full salute

Later on we smoked a pipe that struck me dumb
And made it impossible to speak
As you closed in, in slow motion
Quoting Sappho, in the original Greek

She moves among the shadows
She floats upon the breeze
She moves among the candles
And we moved through the days and through the years

Years passed by, we were walking by the sea
Half delirious
You smiled at me and said, babe
I think this thing is getting kind of serious
You pointed at something and said
Have you ever seen such a beautiful thing?
It was then that I broke down
It was then that you lifted me up again

She moves among the sparrows
And she walks across the sea
She moves among the flowers
And she moves something deep inside of me

She moves among the sparrows
And she floats upon the breeze
She moves among the flowers
And she moves right up close to me

Abattoir Blues

The sun is high up in the sky and I'm in my car
Drifting down into the abattoir
Do you see what I see, dear?

The air grows heavy. I listen to your breath
Entwined together in this culture of death
Do you see what I see, dear?

Slide on over here, let me give you a squeeze
To avert this unholy evolutionary trajectory
Can you hear what I hear, babe?
Does it make you feel afraid?

Everything's dissolving, babe, according to plan
The sky is on fire, the dead are heaped across the land
I went to bed last night and my moral code got jammed
I woke up this morning with a Frappuccino in my hand

I kissed you once. I kissed you again
My heart it tumbled like the stock exchange
Do you feel what I feel, dear?

Mass extinction, darling, hypocrisy
These things are not good for me
Do you see what I see, dear?

The line the God throws down to you and me
Makes a pleasing geometry
Shall we leave this place now, dear?
Is there some way out of here?

I wake with the sparrows and I hurry off to work
The need for validation, babe, gone completely berserk
I wanted to be your Superman but I turned out such a jerk
I got the abattoir blues
I got the abattoir blues
I got the abattoir blues
Right down to my shoes

Let the Bells Ring

C'mon, kind Sir, let's walk outside
And breathe the autumn air
See the many that have lived and died
See the unending golden stair
See all of us that come behind
Clutching at your hem
All the way from Arkansas
To your sweet and last amen

Let the bells ring
He is the real thing
Let the bells ring
He is the real, real thing

Take this deafening thunder down
Take this bread and take this wine
Your passing is not what we mourn
But the world you left behind
Well, do not breathe, nor make a sound
And behold your mighty work
That towers over the uncaring ground
Of a lesser, darker world

Let the bells ring
He is the real thing
Let the bells ring
He is the real, real thing

There are those of us not fit to tie
The laces of your shoes
Must remain behind to testify
Through an elementary blues

So, let's walk outside, the hour is late
Through your crumbs and scattered shells
Where the awed and the mediocre wait
Barely fit to ring the bells

Let the bells ring
He is the real thing
Let the bells ring
He is the real, real thing

Fable of the Brown Ape

Farmer Emmerich went into his barn
And found a cow suckling a serpent
And a brown ape clanking a heavy chain
Said Farmer Emmerich to the ape
Never ask me to come into this barn again
So long
Farewell
So long

Farmer Emmerich caught the serpent
And the brown ape in a cage
And took them into his house
He fed the snake a vat of milk
And when the ape rattled its chain
He tossed the ape a mouse
So long
Goodbye
Farewell

The villagers found out that Farmer Emmerich
Was nurturing a serpent
And descended upon his farm
All rabid in their blindness
They dragged the snake outside
Chopped it open with an axe
And the ground soaked
In the milk of human kindness
So long
Farewell
So long

But the brown ape escaped
And was heard to roam the ranges
Clanking its heavy chain
Down in the valley it sang to its friend
Whom he may never see again

The Lyre of Orpheus

Orpheus sat gloomy in his garden shed
Wondering what to do
With a lump of wood, a piece of wire
And a little pot of glue
O Mamma O Mamma

He sawed at the wood with half a heart
And glued it top to bottom
He strung a wire in between
He was feeling something rotten
O Mamma O Mamma

Orpheus looked at his instrument
And he gave the wire a pluck
He heard a sound so beautiful
He gasped and said, O my God
O Mamma O Mamma

He rushed inside to tell his wife
He went racing down the halls
Eurydice was still asleep in bed
Like a sack of cannonballs
O Mamma O Mamma

Look what I've made, cried Orpheus
And he plucked a gentle note
Eurydice's eyes popped from their sockets
And her tongue burst through her throat
O Mamma O Mamma

O God, what have I done, he said
As her blood pooled in the sheets
But in his heart he felt a bliss
With which nothing could compete
O Mamma O Mamma

Orpheus went leaping through the fields
Strumming as hard as he did please
Birdies detonated in the sky
Bunnies dashed their brains out on the trees
O Mamma O Mamma

Orpheus strummed till his fingers bled
He hit a G minor 7
He woke up God from a deep, deep sleep
God was a major player in heaven
O Mamma O Mamma

God picked up a giant hammer
And He threw it with a thunderous yell
It smashed down hard on Orpheus' head
And knocked him down a well
O Mamma O Mamma

The well went down very deep
Very deep went down the well
The well went down so very deep
Well, the well went down to hell
O Mamma O Mamma

Poor Orpheus woke up with a start
All amongst the rotting dead
His lyre tucked safe under his arm
His brains all down his head
O Mamma O Mamma

Eurydice appeared brindled in blood
And she said to Orpheus
If you play that fucking thing down here
I'll stick it up your orifice!
O Mamma O Mamma

This lyre lark is for the birds, said Orpheus
It's enough to send you bats
Let's stay down here, Eurydice, dear
And we'll have a bunch of screaming brats
O Mamma O Mamma

Orpheus picked up his lyre for the last time
He was on a real low-down bummer
And stared deep into the abyss and said
This one is for Mamma

O Mamma O Mamma
O Mamma O Mamma
O Mamma O Mamma
O Mamma O Mamma

Breathless

It's up in the morning and on the downs
Little white clouds like gambolling lambs
And I am breathless over you
And the red-breasted robin beats his wings
His throat it trembles when he sings
For he is helpless before you
The happy hooded bluebells bow
And bend their heads all a-down
Heavied by the early-morning dew
At the whispering stream, at the bubbling brook
The fishes leap up to take a look
For they are breathless over you
Still your hands
And still your heart
For still your face comes shining through
And all the morning glows anew
Still your mind
Still your soul
For still, the fire of love is true
And I am breathless without you

The wind circles among the trees
And it bangs about the new-made leaves
For it is breathless without you
The fox chases the rabbit round
The rabbit hides beneath the ground
For he is defenceless without you
The sky of daytime dies away
And all earthly things, they stop to play
For we are all breathless without you
I listen to my juddering bones
The blood in my veins and the wind in my lungs

And I am breathless without you
Still your hands
And still your heart
For still your face comes shining through
And all the morning glows anew
Still your soul
Still your mind
Still, the fire of love is true
And I am breathless without you

Babe, You Turn Me On

Stay by me, stay by me
You are the one, my only true love

The butcher bird makes its noise
And asks you to agree
With its brutal nesting habits
And its pointless savagery
Now, the nightingale sings to you
And raises up the ante
I put one hand on your round ripe heart
And the other down your panties

Everything is falling, dear
Everything is wrong
It's just history repeating itself
And babe, you turn me on

Like a light bulb
Like a song

You race naked through the wilderness
You torment the birds and the bees
You leaped into the abyss, but find
It only goes up to your knees
I move stealthily from tree to tree
I shadow you for hours
I make like I'm a little deer
Grazing on the flowers

Everything is collapsing, dear
All moral sense has gone
It's just history repeating itself
And babe, you turn me on

Like an idea
Like an atom bomb

We stand awed inside a clearing
We do not make a sound
The crimson snow falls all about
Carpeting the ground

Everything is falling, dear
All rhyme and reason gone
It's just history repeating itself
And babe, you turn me on

Like an idea
Like an atom bomb

Easy Money

It's difficult. It's very tough
I said to the man who'd been sleeping rough
To sit within a fragrant breeze
All among the nodding trees
That hang heavy with the stuff

He threw his arms around my neck
He brushed the tear from my cheek
And held my soft white hand
He was an understanding man
He did not even barely hardly speak

Easy money
Rain it down on the wife and the kids
Rain it down on the house where we live
Rain until you got nothing left to give
And rain that ever-loving stuff down on me

All the things for which my heart yearns
Gives joy in diminishing returns
He kissed me on the mouth
His hands they headed south
And my cheek, it burned

Money, man, it is a bitch
The poor, they spoil it for the rich
With my face pressed in the clover
I wondered when this would be over
And at home we are all so guilty-sad

Easy money
Pour it down the open drain
Pour it all through my veins
Pour it down, yeah, let it rain
And pour that ever-loving stuff down on me

Now, I'm sitting pretty down on the bank
Life shuffles past at a low interest rate
In the money-coloured meadows
And all the interesting shadows
They leap up, then dissipate

Easy money
Easy money
Easy money
Rain it down on the wife and the kids
Rain it down on the house where we live
Rain it down until you got nothing left to give
And rain that ever-loving stuff down on me

Supernaturally

Through the windswept coastal trees
Where the dead come rising from the sea
With a teddy-bear clamped between her knees
She says, where can my loverman be?
Well, I'm down here, babe, with the Eskimos
With the polar bears and the Arctic snow
With a party of penguins who do not know
How I can get back to thee
Well, I'm gonna ask you, babe
Hey! Ho!
Oh baby, don't you go
Hey! Ho!
Oh no no no
Hey! Ho!
Oh baby, don't you go
All supernatural on me
Supernaturally

Once I was your heart's desire
Now I'm the ape hunkered by the fire
With my knuckles dragging through the mire
You float by so majestically
You're my north, my south, my east, my west
You are the girl that I love best
With an army of tanks bursting from your chest
I wave my little white flag at thee
Can you see it, babe?
Hey! Ho!
Oh baby, don't you go
Hey! Ho!
Oh no no no
Hey! Ho!

Oh baby, don't you go
All supernatural on me
Supernaturally

Now I've turned the mirrors to wall
I've emptied out the peopled halls
I've nailed shut the windows and locked the doors
There is no escape, you see
I chase you up and down the stairs
Under tables and over chairs
I reach out and I touch your hair
And it cuts me like a knife
For there is always some other little thing you gotta do
Hey! Ho!
Oh baby, don't you go
Hey! Ho!
Oh baby, no no no
Hey! Ho!
Oh don't you go
All supernatural on me
Supernaturally

Spell

Through the woods and frosted moors
Past the snow-caked hedgerows I
Bed down upon the drifting snow
Sleep beneath the melting sky
I whisper all your names
I know not where you are
But somewhere, somewhere, somewhere here
Upon this wild abandoned star

And I'm full of love
And I'm full of wonder
And I'm full of love
And I'm falling under
Your spell

I have no abiding memory
No awakening, no flaming dart
No word of consolation
No arrow through my heart
Only a feeble notion
A glimmer from afar
That I cling to with my fingers
As we go spinning wildly through the stars

And I'm full of love
And I'm full of wonder
And I'm full of love
And I'm falling under
Your spell

The wind lifts me to my senses
I rise up with the dew
The snow turns to streams of light
The purple heather grows anew
I call you by your name
I know not where you are
But somehow, somewhere, sometime soon
Upon this wild abandoned star

And I'm full of love
And I'm full of wonder
And I'm full of love
And I'm falling under
Your spell

Carry Me

I lay down by the river
The shadows moved across me, inch by inch
And all I heard
Was the war between the water and the bridge
Turn to me, turn to me, turn to me
Turn and drink of me
Or look away, look away, look away
And never more think of me

Carry me
Carry me

I heard the many voices
Speaking to me from the depths below
This ancient wound
This catacomb
Beneath the whited snow
Come to me, come to me, come to me
Come and drink of me
Or turn away, turn away, turn away
And never more think of me

Carry me
Carry me away

Who will lay down their hammer?
Who will put up their sword?
And pause to see
The mystery
Of the Word

Carry me
Carry me
Carry me
Carry me away
Carry me
Carry me
Carry me
Carry me away

O Children

Pass me that lovely little gun
My dear, my darling one
The cleaners are coming, one by one
You don't even want to let them start

They are knocking now upon your door
They measure the room, they know the score
They're mopping up the butcher's floor
Of your broken little hearts

O children

Forgive us now for what we've done
It started out as a bit of fun
Here, take these before we run away
The keys to the gulag

O children
Lift up your voice, lift up your voice
Children
Rejoice, rejoice

Here comes Frank and poor old Jim
They're gathering round with all my friends
We're older now, the light is dim
And you are only just beginning

O children

We have the answer to all your fears
It's short, it's simple, it's crystal clear
It's round about, it's somewhere here
Lost amongst our winnings

O children
Lift up your voice, lift up your voice
Children
Rejoice, rejoice

The cleaners have done their job on you
They're hip to it, man, they're in the groove
They've hosed you down, you're good as new
They're lining up to inspect you

O children

Poor old Jim's white as a ghost
He's found the answer that was lost
We're all weeping now, weeping because
There ain't nothing we can do to protect you

O children
Lift up your voice, lift up your voice
Children
Rejoice, rejoice

Hey, little train! We are all jumping on
The train that goes to the Kingdom
We're happy, Ma, we're having fun
And the train ain't even left the station

Hey, little train! Wait for me!
I once was blind but now I see
Have you left a seat for me?
Is that such a stretch of the imagination?

Hey, little train! Wait for me!
I was held in chains but now I'm free
I'm hanging in there, don't you see
In this process of elimination

Hey, little train! We are all jumping on
The train that goes to the Kingdom
We're happy, Ma, we're having fun
It's beyond my wildest expectation

Hey, little train! We are all jumping on
The train that goes to the Kingdom
We're happy, Ma, we're having fun
And the train ain't even left the station

She's Leaving You

You were planning to stay in, you had it carefully planned
Your coat was hanging in the hall, your hat was in your hand
You walked over to your woman, your pale distracted love
Who was trying to put the wrong hand into the wrong glove

Are you leaving, dear? Are you leaving, dear?
Are you leaving, dear? Are you leaving, dear?

So you start reading all her books, all her magazines
Just to get a better understanding
Your brain feels like it's dead
Your eyes are hanging out your head
You were hoping for something less demanding
Well what you see staring out at you from a photo book
A man with an eyepatch and a bent, bloody hook
You wished to God that you never went and took a look
Cause it's in that moment that you know that

She's leaving you
Yeah she's leaving you

Well now she's taking you to bed
Her legs wrapped round your head
You're losing her to some crazy kind of motion
You keep coming up for air
You look around and stare
Find you're swimming in two completely different oceans
You're wondering if she's thinking about some other man
She says, 'C'mon, baby, you know you are my loverman'
You're going nuts you don't know exactly what to say
She says, 'Don't worry, baby, this is just my little way'

Of leaving you
Oh, man, she's leaving you

She keeps saying, 'Hey, don't hate me'
She keeps saying, 'Hate is just some kind of failure of the imagination'
She keeps saying things like this
Now she's giving you a kiss
Now she's got you driving her to the station

The sun just slipped out of the sky, this is a black letter day
Her train is moving down the platform, and it is drawing away
You're crying buckets, she gives her glove a wave
She says 'Oh, c'mon, baby, that's no way to behave
when I'm leaving you'

Oh yeah, she's leaving you
Oh yeah, she's leaving you
Yeah, she's leaving you
She's leaving you
Yeah, she's leaving you
Yeah, she's leaving you
Yeah, she's leaving you

Under This Moon

It's been a pleasure, dear
To find your treasure here
And scatter it across the sand

Heaps of coins and ruby rings
And a yellow bird that sings
Songs of sorrow
To your man

Well stand back from that window sill
I'm not holding you here against your will

Well I'm just trying my best to heal
This crazy old moon

It's alright under this moon tonight
With you, dear
It's alright under this moon tonight

Your mouth is a crimson boat
In which my kisses float
In silence to the sea
Oh well I love your touch
I love it very much
Deliriously

Your lover just called
He's on the phone
I'm telling him kindly
That you're not alone
Your smiling eyes
Shine like precious stones
Falling from the sky

It's alright under these stars tonight
With you, baby, it's alright
Under these stars tonight

Let's get it on
And furthermore and in conjunction
And in some other time and space
Well, all joy will come
To you to me to everyone
Oh, babe, didn't we have it made?

Well love is sweet it is agreed
As we float in the shallows in the deep
And on a bed of seaweed sleep
Among the pebbles and the sand

Well it's alright
Under this moon tonight
With you, it's alright
Under this moon tonight

Music from *The Proposition*
(Soundtrack from the Film, 2005)

The Rider
Clean Hands, Dirty Hands

The Rider

Part 1

'When?' said the moon to the stars in the sky
'Soon,' said the wind that followed him home
'Who?' said the cloud that started to cry
'Me,' said the rider as dry as a bone
'How?' said the sun that melted the ground
'Why?' said the river that refused to run
'Where?' said the thunder without a sound
'Here,' said the rider and took up his gun

Part 2

'No,' said the stars to the moon in the sky
'No,' said the trees that started to moan
'No,' said the dust that blinded his eyes
'Yes,' said the rider as white as a bone
'No,' said the moon that rose from his sleep
'No,' said the shriek of the dying sun
'No,' said the planets that started to weep
'Yes,' said the rider and pointed his gun

Part 3

'Goodnight,' said the shadows that started to creep
'Goodnight,' said the sparrow in its bed it did make
'Goodnight,' said the roses that folded asleep
'Goodnight,' said the rider all wide awake
'Good day,' said the bird in the branch of a tree

‘Hello,’ said a snake to the damp night
‘Hello,’ said the fish in their river of sleep
‘Goodbye,’ said the rider. ‘Goodbye and goodnight’

Clean Hands, Dirty Hands

Clean hands and dirty hands, brown eyes and blue
Pale cheeks and rosy cheeks, Jesus loves you
If you come to Him today, He will wash your tears away
Clean hands and dirty hands, brown eyes and blue

Grinderman
(2007)

Get It On
No Pussy Blues
Electric Alice
Grinderman
Depth Charge Ethel
Go Tell the Women
(I Don't Need You To) Set Me Free
Honey Bee (Let's Fly to Mars)
Man In The Moon
When My Love Comes Down
Love Bomb

Chain of Flowers

Get It On

I've got to get up to get down and start all over again
Head on down to the basement and shout
Kick those white mice and black dogs out
Kick those white mice and baboons out
Kick those baboons and other motherfuckers out
And get it on
Get it on
On the day that you got born

They had to dig him from the ground
They chipped him from the frozen snow
They dug his monkey fingers
But he had nowhere to go
They dug his pink hair curlers
They dug his sequinned gown
They dug his Stratocaster
They dug his pornographic crown
He's got some words of wisdom
I got some words of wisdom
He's got some words of wisdom
I got some words of wisdom
Get it on
Get it on
On the day that you got born

He crawled out of the ooze
He defied evolution
He had green flippers and sang the blues
He caused a revolution
He got in the British weeklies
He got in the dailies too
He drank panther piss

And fucked the girls you're probably married to
He's got some words of wisdom
I got some words of wisdom
He's got some words of wisdom
I got some words of wisdom
Get it on
Get it on
On the day that you got born
Get it on
Get it on
Get it on

You gotta do the Vaughan
Well, Papa's down
Yes Sweets is sweet
And Tex is on

Then one day he went away
His neighbour claimed he'd shot him
If he hadn't have disappeared
The taxman would have got him
And so before I leave
I call out from the storm
For those who gave their lives
So we could get it on
Get it on
Get it on
On the day that you got born

No Pussy Blues

My face is finished
My body's gone
And I can't help but think standing up here in all this
applause
And gazing down at all the young and the beautiful
With their questioning eyes
That I must above all things love myself
That I must above all things love myself
That I must above all things love myself

I saw a girl in the crowd
I ran over, I shouted out
I asked if I could take her out
But she said that she didn't want to

I changed the sheets on my bed
I combed the hairs across my head
I sucked in my gut and still she said
That she just didn't want to

I read her Elliott, I read her Yeats
I tried my best to stay up late
I fixed the hinges on her gate
But still she just never wanted to

I bought her a dozen snow-white doves
I did her dishes in rubber gloves
I called her Honey Bee, I called her Love
But she just still didn't want to
She just never wants to

Damn!

I sent her every type of flower
I played her guitar by the hour
I patted her revolting little Chihuahua
But still she just didn't want to

I wrote a song with a hundred lines
I picked a bunch of dandelions
I walked her through the trembling pines
But she just even then didn't want to
She just never wants to

I thought I'd try another tack
I drank a litre of cognac
I threw her down upon her back
But she just laughed
And said she just didn't want to

I thought I'd have another go
I called her my little ho
I felt like Marcel Marceau must feel
When she said that she just never wanted to
She just didn't want to

I got the no pussy blues
I got the no pussy blues
I got the no pussy blues
Wo! Damn!

Electric Alice

Don't the stars look good tonight?
Thought Electric Alice in the pale moonlight
Don't the moon look big and bright?
Thought Electric Alice in the pale moonlight

I think I hear a baby cry
Thought Electric Alice as she passed by
Makes me feel like I'm a little child again
Thought Electric Alice in the silver rain

Grinderman

I'm the Grinderman
In the silver rain
In the pale moonlight
I am open late
Yes I'm the Grinderman
Seven days a week
In the pale moonlight
In the silver rain
I'm the Grinderman
Any way I can
In the silver rain
In the pale moonlight
Yes I'm the Grinderman
Yes I am
In the silver rain
In the pale moonlight
I am open late
Yes I'm the Grinderman, yes I am
In the silver rain
In the pale moonlight
I am open late
Yes I'm the Grinderman, yes I am
Any way I can
Yes I am

Depth Charge Ethel

I entered the room and the canned laughter
Ethel was angled across some dude's knee
I offered to clothe her, to feed and bath her
If she would give me a little exclusivity
Yeah Depth Charge Ethel
Is something special
Yeah Depth Charge Ethel
Is special to me

Ethel is a woman that a river runs through
She is famous throughout the land
People come and bathe in her, yeah, you know I do
But lately it's getting right out of hand
Yeah Depth Charge Ethel
Is something special
Yeah Depth Charge Ethel
Is something special to me

To kiss Ethel is like drinking the stars
But to not kiss her can make you come unglued
So if you want a piece of her you better get in there fast
Right now there is a ticket box and a queue
Depth Charge Ethel
Is something special
Yeah Depth Charge Ethel
Is something special to me

Depth Charge Ethel thinks we should all just take a chance
We should all love one another, it could be special
I'm in the back of the taxi cab with ants in my pants
(I can't sit still), I know they're going to send me

Depth Charge Ethel
She's something special
Yeah Depth Charge Ethel is something special
Yeah Depth Charge Ethel is heavy metal
Yeah Heavy Metal
Yeah Depth Charge Ethel is something special to me

Go Tell The Women

We've done our thing
We have evolved
We're up on our hind legs
The problem's solved
We are artists
We are mathematicians
Some of us hold extremely
High positions
But we are tired
We're hardly breathing
And we're free
Go tell the women that we're leaving

We're sick and tired
Of all this self-serving grieving
All we wanted was a little consensual rape in the afternoon
And maybe a bit more in the evening
We are scientists
We do genetics
We leave religion
To the psychos and fanatics
But we are tired
We've got nothing to believe in
We are lost
Go tell the women that we are leaving

We've done our thing
We're hip to the sound
Of six billion people
Going down

We are magicians
We are deceiving
We're free and we're lost
Go tell the women that we're leaving

Come on back now to the fray
Come on back now to the fray

(I Don't Need You To) Set Me Free

I saw you walking down on the street
I called out from my window but you didn't hear me
I lay down and I try to sleep
I waited for you to walk on by again
I don't need you to set me free
I don't want you to set me free

Well every time I see you I get sick
And every time I think of you I get sick
And every time I dream of you I get sick
And every time I cry for you I get sick
I don't want you to set me free
I don't need you to set me free

Set me free
Set me free
Set me free
Set me free

Honey Bee (Let's Fly To Mars)

Mad mullahs and dirty bombs
Alert the coastal command
Ack-ack positions everyone
She's my honey bee and here she comes
Cancer, rabies, SARS
Hairy beards and hurtling stars
Won't somebody touch me?
Won't somebody touch me?
Honey bee let's fly to Mars
Honey bee let's fly to Mars
Honey bee let's fly to Mars
Honey bee let's fly to Mars
Buzz Buzz

There's a kid laying on the lawn
The neighbour's on the telephone
The dispatcher asked 'what's goin on?'
'Please sir, what's going on?'
The kid is laying on the lawn
He's been giving me shit for years
He rides his bike across the lawn
Now he's laying on the lawn
Won't somebody touch me?
Honey bee let's fly to Mars
Honey bee let's fly to Mars
Honey bee let's fly to Mars
Honey bee let's fly to Mars
Buzz Buzz

Scud missiles, Asian flu
The easily offended
We are the undefended
We are the undefended
Won't somebody touch us?
There's a virus come to town
Won't somebody give me a kiss?
He's been giving me shit for years
Honey bee let's fly to Mars
Honey bee let's fly to Mars
Honey bee let's fly to Mars
Honey bee let's fly to Mars
Honey bee
Honey bee
Buzz Buzz

Man in the Moon

My daddy was an astronaut
That's what I was often taught
My daddy went away too soon
Now he's living on the moon
Hang onto me people
We're going down
Down among the fishes
In an absence of sound
It's the presence of distance
And it's floating in time
It's lack and it's longing
And it's not very kind
Sitting here scratching
In this rented room
Scratching and a tapping
To the man in the moon
About all the things
That I've been taught
My daddy was an astronaut

When My Love Comes Down

When my love comes down to meet you
When my love comes down to meet you again
When my love comes down to meet you
When my love comes down to meet you again

Your mouth is a hologram
Made of spider's bones
Your fingers little soldiers drumming
On their way back home
I thought I saw a thundercloud
On the avenue
Lightning rattled through the streets
That little storm was you

When my love comes down to meet you
When my love comes down to meet you again

Your skin is like the falling snow
Your hair is like the rising sun
Your tongue is like a Kalashnikov
Or some other foreign gun
I see you standing there
Way down upon the street
Marching victorious
With your banners of defeat

When my loves comes down to meet you
When my love comes down to meet you again
When my love comes down to meet you
When my love comes down to meet you again

When my love comes down to meet you
When my love comes down to meet you again
When my love comes down to meet you
When my love comes down to meet you again

Love Bomb

I read the book from back to front
It made a deep impression
Yeah, twenty thousand pages baby
And I hoped for some direction
I stood before the mirror
And I stared at my reflection
I'd almost disappeared
And I made no impression
I went down to my baby's house
And I sat down on the stair
Said two thousand years of Christian history baby
And you ain't learned to love me yet
My baby looked me in the eye
My nails were bitten to the quick
She said you used to love me all night long
But you've gotten so thin and sick

Gonna send you
A love bomb
Gonna send you
A love bomb

I read the book from back to front
Looking for some inspiration
I been listening to the radio
Trying to find some self-expression
I been listening to the Woman's Hour
I been listening to Gardeners' Question Time
But everything I try to grow
I can't even grow a dandelion
I been watching the MTV
I been watching the BBC

I been searching on the Internet
I'm getting so thin and sick

I'm gonna send you
A love bomb
I'm gonna send you
A love bomb

I went to my baby's house
I sat down on the step
I went down to my baby's house
And I lay down on her step
She said what are you doing here?
I said I been trying to make some sense
But every action that I try to take
Is of absolutely no consequence
My baby said you can't sit there
She reached down with her fingers
Her fingers went right through me
I screamed my head off
I was so thin and sick

I'm gonna send you
A love bomb
I'm gonna send you
A love bomb

Chain of Flowers

I know you're hanging around outside my door
I know you've been here six times today, or maybe more
I know you're hesitating
But I'm here waiting
Don't you know it'll be alright
Don't you know it'll be alright

Maybe you can become a friend of mine
Every time you come around here you leave a dandelion
And I've been sitting here for hours
Making a chain of flowers
Don't you know it'll be alright
Don't you know it'll be alright

The chains of flowers are fragile things
They break in time
But the chains of love are the chains of love are the chains that bind
The chains of flowers are fragile things
They break in time
But the chains of love are the chains of love are the chains of love

People keep telling me I'm lonely
That I'd be happy if you'd only
Throw that door open wide
And step inside
And everything will be alright
And everything will be alright
Yeah, everything will be alright

DIG, LAZARUS, DIG!!!
(2008)

DIG, LAZARUS, DIG!!!

Today's Lesson
Moonland
Night of the Lotus Eaters
Albert Goes West
We Call Upon the Author
Hold On to Yourself
Lie Down Here (& Be My Girl)
Jesus of the Moon
Midnight Man
More News from Nowhere

DIG, LAZARUS, DIG!!!

dig yourself, LAZARUS!!!!!!
DIG YOURSELF, LAZARUS!!!!!!!!!!!!!!!!!!!
dig yourself, LAZARUS!!!!!!!!
(dig yourself back in that hole)
Larry made his nest up in the autumn branches
built from nothing but high hopes & thin air
he collected up some BABY-BLASTED mothers
they took their chances
& for a while lived quite happily up there
he came from NEW YORK CITY, but he couldn't take the pace
(thought it was like DOGGY-DOG-WORLD)
then he went to SAN FRANCISCO
(spent a year in outer space)
w/ a sweet little san franciscan girl
I can hear my mother wailing
& a whole lot of scraping of chairs!!!!!!!!
I don't know what it is
but there is definitely something going on upstairs
dig yourself, LAZARUS!!!!!!
DIG YOURSELF, LAZARUS!!!!!!!!!!!!!!!!!!!
dig yourself, LAZARUS!!!!!!!!
(dig yourself back in that hole)
I!!!! WANT!!!!! Y/!!!!!!!! TO!!!!!!!! DIG!!!!!!!!!!!!!!!!!!!
yeah, NEW YORK CITY, he had to get out of there
& san francisco, well, I don't know
& then to LA, where he spent about a day
he thought even the pale sky-stars
were smart enough to keep well away
from LA!!!!!!

meanwhile Larry made up names for the ladies, like
MISS BOO!!!! & MISS QUICK!!!!!!!
he stockpiled weapons & took pot shots at the air
he feasted on their lovely bodies like a lunatic
wrapped himself up in their soft yellow hair

I can hear chants & incantations
& some guy is mentioning me in his prayers!!!!!
I don't know what it is
but there is definitely something going on upstairs
dig yourself, LAZARUS!!!!!!
DIG YOURSELF, LAZARUS!!!!!!!!!!!!!!!!!!
dig yourself, LAZARUS!!!!!!!!
(dig yourself back in that hole)
I!!!! WANT!!!!! Y/!!!!!!!! TO!!!!!!!! DIG!!!!!!!!!!!!!!!!!!
well NEW YORK CITY, man
SAN FRANCISCO, LA (I don't know)
Larry grew increasingly neurotic & obscene!!!!!!!!
HE NEVER ASKED TO BE RAISED UP FROM
THE TOMB!!!
no one ever actually asked him to forsake his DREAMS!!!
anyway, to cut a long story short
fame finally found him
mirrors became his torturers
cameras snapped him at every chance
the women all went back to their homes
& their husbands
(secret smiles in the corners of their mouths)
he ended up like so many of them do
back on the streets of
NEW YORK CITY!!!!!!!!! (crowd) !!!!!!!!!!!!!!!!!!!!!!
in a soup queue/
a dope fiend/ (a slave)
then prison/ then the madhouse/
then the grave

O POOR LARRY!!!!!!!!!!!!!!!!!!!!!!!!!!!!!!!!!!
but what do we really know of the dead
& who actually cares???????????!!!!!
I don't know what it is
but there is definitely something going on upstairs
dig yourself, LAZARUS!!!!!!

DIG YOURSELF, LAZARUS!!!!!!!!!!!!!!!!!!
dig yourself, LAZARUS!!!!!!!!
(dig yourself back in that hole)
I!!!! WANT!!!!! Y/!!!!!!!! TO!!!!!!!! DIG!!!!!!!!!!!!!!!!!!

Today's Lesson

Little Janie she wakes up from a dream
    a gun like a jawbone down the waistb& of her jeans
mr Sandman can recite today's lesson in his sleep
he says
    (there oughta be a law against me going down on the street)
little Janie pipes up & she says!!!!!
        we're GONNA HAVE A REAL COOL TIME
            TONITE!!!!
down the back of Janie's jeans she had the jawbone of an ass
            mr Sandman runs around the corner
trying to head her off at the pass
he sticks his head over the fence and yells
something way too fast
                    (it's today's lesson)
something about the
        CORRUPTION OF THE WORKING CLASS!!!!
little Janie wakes up on the floor & she says!!!!
        we're GONNA HAVE A REAL COOL TIME
            TONITE!!!!
(Janie says we are all such a crush of want half-mad w/ loss we are
violated in our sleep & we weep & we toss & we turn & we burn we are
hypnotised we are cross-eyed we are pimped we are bitched we are told such monstrous lies---)

Janie wakes up & she says
        we're GONNA HAVE A REAL COOL TIME
            TONITE!!!!
mr Sandman has a certain appetite for Janie in repose

he digs her pretty knees & that she is completely naked
underneath all her clothes
he likes to congregate around the intersection of Janie's jeans

mr Sandman   the inseminator
opens her up like a love-letter   & enters her   dreams
little Janie wakes up & she says!!!!
we're GONNA HAVE A REAL good TIME
TONITE!!!!
o yeah little Janie wakes up & she says!!!!
we're GONNA HAVE A REAL good TIME
TONITE!!!!
TONITE!!!! TONITE!!!! TONITE!!!!! CMON!!!!
CMON!!!!
CMON!!!!
CMON!!!!!
CMON!!!!!!!

Moonland

when I came up from out of the meat-locker
the city was gone
the sky was full of lights
the snow provides a silent cover
in moonland, under the stars
under the s&, I followed this car
& I followed that car, through the s&
through the snow, I turn on the radio
I listen to the deejay, & it must feel nice
it must feel nice to know, that somebody needs you
& everything moves slow, under the stars
under the ash, through the s&
& the night drifts in, the snow provides a silent cover
& I'm not your favourite lover, I turn on the radio
& it must feel nice
o very very nice to know, that somebody needs you
& the chilly winds blow, under the snow
under the stars, the whispering deejay
on the radio, the whispering deejay
on the radio, I'm not yr favourite lover
I'm not yr favourite lover, & It must feel nice
to leave no trace (no trace at all)
but somebody needs you, and that somebody is me
under the stars, under the snow
(yr eyes were closed
you were playing w/ the buttons on yr coat
in the back of that car)
in moonl&, under the stars
in moonl&, & I followed that car

Night of the Lotus Eaters

sapped & stupid
I lie upon the stones and I swoons
the darling little dandelions have done their thing
& changed from suns into moons
the dragons roam the shopping malls
I hear theyre gonna eat our guts
if I had the strength I might pick up my sword
& make some attempt to resist
get ready to shield yourself!!!!!!!!!
grab yr sap & yr heaters
get ready to shield yourself!!!!!!!!!
on the night of the lotus eaters
mmmmmmmm don't you love my baby
mmmmmmmm & don't you love my baby anymore
they gilded my scales/ they fish-bowled me
& they toured me round the old aquariums
they come in their hordes to tap at the glass
the philistines and barbarians
I like
floating
here (it's nice)
theyve hung seaweed round my hips
& I do the
<<hula>>
for the hungry ones
& the lames all throw me tips
get ready to shield yourself!!!!!!!!!
grab yr sap & yr heaters
get ready to shield yourself!!!!!!!!!
on the night of the lotus eaters

mmmmmmmm don't you love my baby
mmmmmmmm & don't you love my baby anymore
get ready to shield yourself!!!!!!!!!
from our catastrophic leaders

get ready to shield yourself!!!!!!!!!
grab yr sap & yr heaters
on the night of the lotus eaters
now hit the streets!!!!!!!
Now
        HIT
                    the
                        streets!!!!!!!!!!!!!!!!!!!!!!!!!!!

Albert Goes West

albert he goes west/ he crossed
the vast indifferent deserts of Arizona

he had a psychotic episode on a dude ranch
that involved a bottle of ammonia

henry he went south & lost his way
deep in the weeping forests of le vulva

he grew so wan/ he grew so sick
he ended up in a bungalow/ sucking a revolver

the light upon yr rainy streets
offers many reflections

& I wont be held responsible
for my actions

bobby he goes north/ then goes east
then over to new Hampshire
bobby is a cautious man/ he walked into
a Concord dive/ to drink a beer

do you wanna dance????!!!!
do you wanna move????!!!!

do you wanna dance????!!!!
do you wanna GROOVE????!!!!

the world is full of
endless abstractions

& I wont be held responsible
for my actions

me/ I aint going anywhere
just sit & watch the sun come up/ I like it here!!!

I watch the people go ticking past/ I go hey hey hey
you know I gotta say/ I like it here!!!

sha-la-la-la   sha la-la-la   sha-la-la-la-la-la-la-la!!!

sha-la-la-la   sha la-la-la   sha-la-la-la-la-la-la-la!!!

We Call Upon the Author

what we once thought we had we didnt
            & what we have now will never be that way again
      so WE CALL UPON THE AUTHOR TO EXPLAIN!!!
doop doop doop doop doop doop doop &tc
our myxomatoid kids spraddle the streets
                weve shunned them from the greasy-grind
(the poor little things)
                they look so sad & old
as they mount us from behind
I ask them to desist
                & to
                      REFRAIN!!!!!!!!!!!!!!!
      then WE CALL UPON THE AUTHOR TO EXPLAIN!!!
doop doop doop doop doop doop doop &tc
(rosary clutched in his h&
he died w/ tubes up his nose
& a cabal of angels w/ finger cymbals
chanted his name in code)
we shook our fists at the punishing rain
        & WE CALLED UPON THE AUTHOR TO EXPLAIN!!!!!
doop doop doop doop doop doop doop &tc
he said --- everything is messed up round here / everything is banal
and jejune / there is a planetary conspiracy / against the likes of you
& me / in this idiot
constituency of the moon---
            (well, he knew exactly who to blame!!!!)
      & WE CALL UPON THE AUTHOR TO EXPLAIN!!!!!
doop doop doop doop doop doop doop &tc
PROLIX!!!!
      PROLIX!!!!
            NOTHING A PAIR OF SCISSORS CAN'T FIX!!!!

doop doop doop doop doop doop doop &tc
doop doop doop doop doop doop doop &tc
I go guruing down the street
young people gather round my feet
ask me things – but I don't know where to start
they ignite the powder-trail sssssstraight to my father's heart!!!!!
& once again
I CALL UPON THE AUTHOR TO EXPLAIN!!!!!!!
doop doop doop doop doop doop doop &tc
(we call upon the author to explain)
who is this great burdensome slavering dog-thing that
mediocres my every thought???
I feel like a VACUUM CLEANER!!! A COMPLETE SUCKER!!!!
(it's fucked up & he is a fucker!)
but what an enormous & encyclopaedic brain!!!!!!!!!!
I CALL UPON THE AUTHOR TO EXPLAIN!!!!!!
doop doop doop doop doop doop &tc
(mmm yeah)
doop doop doop doop doop &tc
(we call upon the author to explain)
o rampant discrimination/ mass poverty/ third world debt/
infectious
disease/ global inequality and deepening socio-economic
divisions---
(it does in your brain!!!)
WE CALL UPON THE AUTHOR TO EXPLAIN!!!!!!!
doop doop doop doop doop doop doop &tc
now hang on!!! my friend Doug is tapping on the window
(hey Doug, how you been???????????????????)

brings me a book on holocaust poetry
-----complete with pictures-----
then tells me to get ready for the rain
and WE CALL UPON THE AUTHOR TO EXPLAIN!!!!!!!
doop doop doop doop doop doop doop &tc

PROLIX!!!!
PROLIX!!!!
SOMETHING A PAIR OF SCISSORS CAN
FIX!!!!!!!!
Bukowski was a jerk!!!!!!!!!!!!!!!!
Berryman was best!!!!!!!!!!!!
he wrote like wet papier mache/ went the Hemming-way/ weirdly
on wings & with MAXIMUM PAIN!!!
WE CALL UPON THE AUTHOR TO EXPLAIN!!!!!
doop doop doop doop doop doop doop &tc
(I call upon the author to explain!)
down in my bolthole I see they've published
another volume of unreconstructed rubbish
'the waves, the waves were soldiers moving'
thank you! thank you! thank you! & again!
I CALL UPON THE AUTHOR TO EXPLAIN!!!!!
doop doop doop doop doop doop doop &tc
WE CALL UPON THE AUTHOR TO EXPLAIN!!!
doop doop doop doop doop doop doop &tc
WE CALL UPON THE AUTHOR TO EXPLAIN!!!!
doop doop doop doop doop doop doop &tc
PROLIX!!!!
PROLIX!!!!
NOTHING A PAIR OF SCISSORS CAN'T FIX!!!!!!!!

Hold On to Yourself

(I'm so far away from you)
I'm pacing up & down my room
does Jesus only love a man who loses?
I turn on the radio--------
there's some cat on the saxophone
laying down a litany of excuses
there's madhouse longing in my baby's eyes
she rubs the lamp between her thighs
& hopes the genie comes out singing
she lives in some forgotten song
& moves like she is zombie-strong
breathes steady as the pendulum---
keeps swinging
oooooooo you better hold on to yourself
well cities rust & fall to ruin
factories close & cars go cruising
in around the borders of her vision
she says o o o o o o o o o
as Jesus make the flowers grow
all around the scene of her collision
o you know I would / I'd hold on to yourself
in the middle of the night

I try my best to chase outside
the phantoms & the ghosts & fairy-girls
on 1001 nights likes these
she mutters open sesame
& Ali Baba & the forty thieves
launch her off the face of the world
o you know/one day I'll come back/& hold on to yourself
o baby I'm a 1000 miles away

I just don't know what to say
cause Jesus only loves a man who bruises
but darling we can clearly see

it's all life & fire & lunacy
& excuses & excuses & excuses
if I could, I would/ I'd lie right down/ & hold on to yourself
one day I'll come back to you & I'll lie down & I'll hold on to
yourself

Lie Down Here (& Be My Girl)

well y/ lost a foe &
y/ found yrself a friend
(lie down here & be my girl)
I'm back now/ baby / that man
he won't be coming round here again
(lie down here & be my girl)
I'm trying to tread careful/ baby
yr as brittle as the wishbone of a bird
(lie down here & be my girl)
we've been scribbled in the margins
of a story that is patently absurd
(lie down here & be my girl)
& let it all come down
tonight
(& shine & shine)
& let it all come down
(be my girl/ be my girl)
it's a matter of some urgency
o darling can't y/ see/ I can't hold back the tide
(lie down here & be my girl)
& stop yr frantic little fingers trying to collect
the years that pour from the hole in my side
(lie down here & be my girl)
o don't worry baby/ this old snake
banging at yr door has got a few skins left to shed
(lie down here & be my girl)
o y/ look so good/ y/ look so so good
the rest is better left unsaid
(lie down here & be my girl)
let it all come down

tonight
(& shine & we can shine)
let it all come down
tonight (be my girl)

one day I'll buy a factory & I'll assemble y/
on a production line
(lie down here & be my girl)
I'd build a million of y/ baby
& every single one of them will be mine
(lie down here & be my girl)
I will fill the house w/ y/ stack y/ up
in every room/ we'll have a real good time
(lie down here & be my girl)
but right now/ I'm sitting here
on my own/ going out of my mind
(lie down here & be my girl)
let it all come down
tonight
(& shine & shine)
tonight
tonight (be my girl)
y/ look so good
y/ look so good
&tc &tc &tc

Jesus of the Moon

I stepped out of the St. James Hotel
I'd left y/ behind curled up like a child
well, a change is gonna come
& as the door whispered shut
I walked on down the high-windowed hall

y/ lay sleeping on the unmade bed
the weatherman on the television
in the St. James Hotel said
that the rains are gonna come
& I stepped out on the streets/ all sparkling clean
w/ the early morning dew

maybe it was y/ or maybe it was me?
y/ came on like a punch in the heart
y/ lying there w/ the light on yr hair
like a jesus of the moon
a jesus of the planets & the stars

well I kept thinking about what the weatherman said
& if the voices of the living can be heard by the dead
well the day is gonna come
when we find out & in some kinda way
I take a little comfort from that (now & then)

cause people often talk about being scared of change
but for me I'm more afraid of things staying the same
cause the game is never won
by standing in any one place for too long

maybe it was y/ or maybe it was me
but there was a chord in y/ I could not find to strike
y/ lying there w/ all the light in your hair
like a jesus of the moon
a jesus of the planets & the stars

I see the many girls walking down the empty streets
& maybe once or twice one of them smiles at me
y/ can't blame anyone
for saying hello/ I say hey/ I say hello/ I say hello

will it be me or will it be y/?
one must stay & one must depart
y/ lying there in a St. James hotel bed
like a Jesus of the moon
a Jesus of the planets & the stars

I say hello/ hello/ hello

Midnight Man

hold that chrysalis in yr palm
see it split & change
it won't do you any harm
it's just trying to rearrange
it was born to live a day
now it flies up from yr h&
(it's beautiful)
it's the one they call
yr ever-loving man

wolves have carried yr babies away
o yr kids drip from their teeth
the nights are long & the day
is bitter cold beyond belief
you spread yourself like a penitent
upon the mad vibrating s&
& through yr teeth
arrange to meet
yr midnight man

everybody's coming round to my place!!!
everybody's coming round to my place!!!
everybody's coming round!!!
o baby don't y/ see
everybody wants to be
yr midnight man!!!!!

don't disturb me as I sleep
treat me gentle when I wake
don't disturb me as I sleep
even though yr body aches
even though yr body aches

to serve at his comm&
betwn the wars
she still adores
her ever-loving man

close yr eyes, sleep in him
dream of yr lost sons & daughters
me, I'll raise up the dorsal fin
& glide up & down the waters
I'll glide up & down the waters
then I'll walk upon the l&
& call em out
the ones who doubt
yr midnight man

everybody's coming round to my place!!!
everybody's coming round to my place!!!
everybody's coming round!!!
o darling don't y/ see
everybody wants to be
yr midnight man!!!!!

it's early in the morning
& I don't know what to do
it's early in the morning
& I can't believe it's true
it's early in the morning
& it's happening again
I called y/ once
I called y/ twice
ain't I yr midnight man

everybody's coming round to my place!!!
everybody's coming round to my place!!!
everybody's coming round!!!
they want y/
they love y/
they need to be
yr midnight man!!!

everybody's coming round
everybody's coming round
everybody's coming round
everybody's coming round
to be yr midnight man!!!
to be yr midnight man!!!

More News from Nowhere

I walk into the corner of my room
see my friends in high places
I dont know which is which or who is whom
theyve stolen each others faces
Janet is there w/ her hi-hatting hair
full of bedroom feathers
Janet is known to make dead men groan
in any kind of weathers
I crawl over to her
I say –hey baby I say –hey Janet
–you are the one/ you are the sun
& I'm yr dutiful planet–
but she aint down w/ any of that
shes heard that shit before
I say –ah ha o yeah youre right
cause I see Betty X standing by the door
w/ more news from nowhere
more news from nowhere
& its getting strange in here
yeah it gets stranger every year
more news from nowhere
more news from nowhere

now Betty X is like Betty Y
minus that fatal chromosome
her hair is like the wine dark sea
on which sailors come home
I say –hey baby– I say –hey Betty X
(I lean close up to her throat)
–this light you are carrying is like a lamp
hanging from a distant boat

–It is my light– said Betty X
Betty X says –this light aint yours!!!
& so much wind blew through her words

that I went rolling down the hall
for more news from nowhere
more news from nowhere
& its strange in here
yeah it gets stranger every year
more news from nowhere
more news from nowhere

I turn another corner/ I go down a corridor
& I see this guy
he must be about 100 foot tall
& he only has one eye
he asks me for my autograph
I write –nobody– & then
I wrap myself up in my woolly coat
& blind him w/ my pen
cause someone must of stuck something in my drink
everything was getting strange looking
½ the people had turned into squealing pigs
that the other ½ were cooking
–let me out of here!!!– I cried
& I went pushing past
& I saw Miss Polly!!! singing with some girls
I cried, –strap me to the mast!!!!!–
for more news from nowhere
more news from nowhere
its getting strange in here
& it gets stranger every year
more news from nowhere
more news from nowhere

then a black girl w/ no clothes on
danced across the room
we charted the progress of the planets

around that boogie-woogie moon
I called her my nubian princess
I gave her some sweet-back bad-ass jive
I spent the next seven yrs between her legs
pining for my wife
but by and by it all went wrong
I felt all washed-up on the shore
she stared down at me from up in the storm
as I sobbed upon the floor
for more news from nowhere
more news from nowhere
& dont it make you feel alone
& dont it make you wanna get right-on home
more news from nowhere
more news from nowhere

here comes Alina w/ two black eyes
she's given herself a transfusion
she's filled herself w/ panda blood
to avoid all the confusion
I said –the sun rises & falls w/ you–
& various things about love
but a rising violence in me
cut all my circuits off
Alina she starts screaming
her cheeks are full of psychotropic leaves
her extinction was nearly absolute
when she turned her back on me
for more news from nowhere
more news from nowhere

& its getting strange in here
yeah it gets stranger every year
more news from nowhere
more news from nowhere

I bumped bang crash into Deanna
hanging pretty in the door frame
all the horrors that have befallen me
well Deanna is to blame
every time I see you babe
you make me feel so all alone
& I wept my face into her dress
long after she'd gone home
w/ more news from nowhere
more news from nowhere
& dont it make you feel alone
dont it make you wanna get right back home
more news from nowhere
more news from nowhere

dont it make you feel so sad
dont the blood rush to yr feet
to think that everything you do today
tomorrow is obsolete
technology & women
& little children too
dont it make you feel blue
dont it make you feel blue
for more news from nowhere
more news from nowhere
dont it make you feel alone
dont it make you wanna get right back home
more news from nowhere
more news from nowhere

goodbye /goodbye/goodbye

Grinderman 2
(2010)

Mickey Mouse and the Goodbye Man
Worm Tamer
Heathen Child
When My Baby Comes
What I Know
Evil
Kitchenette
Palaces of Montezuma
Bellringer Blues

Mickey Mouse and the Goodbye Man

I woke up this morning and I thought what am I doing
Yeah what am I doing here
I woke up this morning and I thought what am I doing
Yeah what am I doing here
Well my brother, he starts raging!
Watch him rising! See him howling!
And he sucked her and he sucked her and he sucked her dry
And he bit at me and bit at me and said goodbye
Up on the twenty-ninth floor! Up on the twenty-ninth floor!
Aoooooow! Aoooooow!

Well, I was lying there with just my brother
We could hear someone rattling the locks
I was lying there with just my brother
He said do you think that might be the cops?
And we sucked her and we sucked her and we sucked her dry
And we sucked her and we sucked her and we sucked her dry
I was Mickey Mouse! He was the big bad wolf!

Next thing you know I'm looking down below
See a lupine child with her hair on fire
Little burning girl! She's looking up at me!
Running to the elevator! Getting in the elevator!
Sixth floor, seventh floor, eighth floor, nine
Come on baby, gonna blow my mind!
Ooooooow!

Well, I woke up this morning and he was gone
There were posters in the airports and the stations
We took shelter
We took shelter

Under her body
Under her body
We sucked her and we sucked her and we sucked her dry
We sucked her and we sucked her and we shaved her dry
He kissed me and kissed me and said goodbye
He kissed me and kissed me and said goodbye
Alright!

Well, no time at all, she's walking down the hall
She's a bat-faced girl with dynamite curls
Ringing the bell-bell, banging on the door
Walking down the travelator! Walking down the travelator!
Twenny-two twenny-four twenny-six twenny-nine
Come on baby and blow my mind!
Ooooooow! Ooooooooooow! Yeah!

Worm Tamer

You know they call my girl The Snake Charmer
Here she comes rising with the yellow dawn
You know I would do nothing to ever harm her
I guess that I've loved you for too long

You know they call my girl The Worm Tamer
She cracks lightning like a vipers tongue
She leaves me every night and who can blame her
I guess that I've loved you for too long

For too long!
For too long!

You know they call my girl The Serpent Wrangler
Eating inchworms down the bill-a-bong
I spent all last night trying to untangle her
I guess that I've loved you for too long

For too long!
For too long!

You know they call my baby The Mambo Rider
I cry storms of tears till the rising of the dawn
You know I'm only happy when I'm inside her
I guess that I've just loved you for too long

For too long!
For too long!

Well my baby calls me the Loch Ness Monster
Two great big humps and then I'm gone
But actually I am the Abominable Snowman
And I guess I've loved you for too long

Heathen Child

Hey little Moo Moo
Light as a rainbow
Happy as an asteroid
Crashed in the bathtub
Yeah sitting in the bathtub
Full of her fingers
Full of her fingers
Sitting in the bathtub
Says I'm scared and lonely
Never see no one
Says I'm scared and lonely
Here come the Wolfman
Saying hey little Moo Moo
Saying hey little Moo Moo
Sitting in the bathtub

My heathen child
She's a heathen child
She's a heathen child
She's a real wild child

She gotta little powder
She gotta little gun
She gotta little poison, gotta little gun
Sitting in the bathtub sucking her thumb
Says I don't care about Buddha
I don't care about Krishna
I don't care about Allah
I don't care about any of them
Just sitting in the bathtub sucking her thumb

Cause she's a heathen child
She's a heathen child

She's a heathen child
Yeah she's a real wild child

Poor little Moo Moo
Papped and Monroed
She's gotta little powder, gotta lil gun
Sitting in the bathtub having some fun
She was raised by beasts
Photographed by vultures
Here come the Wolfman!
The Abominable Snowman!
Gotta little poison
Gotta little gun
Sitting in the bathtub
Waiting for the Wolfman to come

You think your great big husband will protect you
You are wrong
You think your little wife will protect you
You are wrong
You think your children will protect you
You are wrong
You think your government will protect you
You are wrong
She don't care about Allah
She *is* the Allah
She don't care about Buddah
She *is* the Buddah

She's a heathen child
She's a heathen child
She's a heathen child
She's a real wild child

Down child! Down child!

When My Baby Comes

Thank God we don't get all our hurts
At once that would be a really really bad thing
When my baby comes
Thank God we don't get all our olds at the one time
O listen to me talking in my hospital gown!
When my baby comes
Best thing about this place are the showers
Worst thing is the visiting hours
Hey, careful of the carpet
When my baby comes
They had pistols and they had guns
They threw me on the ground and they entered into me
I was only fifteen
When my baby comes

Just how long you gonna be, my baby?
Just how long you gonna be, my baby?
Until you come?
Just how long you gonna be, my baby?
Just how long you gonna be, my baby?
Until you come?

She got hands as white as milk
And she weaves a loop of spider's silk that glistens
When my baby comes
There is an ancient question behind her eyes
That I can't even begin to describe
Hey, listen don't do that on the carpet!
When my baby comes
Has anyone out there wasted their lives?
On booze and drugs and husbands and wives and making
money?

When my baby comes
Well, they had pistols and they had guns, my skirt above my head
Well, I was so much older when I crawled out
From under their mushroom cloud

Just how long you gonna be, my baby?
Just how long you gonna be, my baby?
Until you come?
Just how long you gonna be, my baby?
Just how long you gonna be, my baby?
Until you come?
Just how long you gonna be, my baby?
Just how long you gonna be, my baby?
Until you come?
When she comes
When she comes

What I Know

Yes, I know
I know
I know it
From the day
That I was born
Yes, I know
From the time
I went to school
Yes, I know
From the time
I was teenager
I know, I know
From the time
I got married
Hey, I know
A million things
Are gonna happen to me
In rooms that are much like this
But it will never be enough
It will never ever be enough
So you better come over here
So you better come over here
So you better come over here
So you better come over here
Cause yeah I know
I know
Never
Ever
No

Evil

O baby, baby, baby!
O my precious baby!

O baby, baby, baby!
Who needs the stars? You are my star!
Who needs the moon? You are my moon!
O baby, baby, baby!

Evil! Evil! Evil! Evil!

Cling to me, baby, in this rented room
Who needs the TV? You are my TV!
Who needs a record player? You are my record player!
O cling to me baby in this rented room

Evil! Evil! Evil! Evil!

Hear the ringing on the telephone
A voice from a hundred miles away
Its breath is heavy and you're all alone
It's got something that it wants to say
It's got something that it wants to say
Its breath is heavy and you're all alone
A voice so clear you can feel its breath
Coming down the telephone

Evil! Evil! Evil! Evil!

O my precious baby
Now is the time that we must speak
They have divided us from our children
And they've tossed them on the heap

Who needs children? You are my child!
Who needs children? My little lamb!
Who needs children! You are my child!
Crying like a demon in your daddy's arms!

Evil! Evil! Evil! Evil!

O cling to me baby in this broken dream
You are the moon! Who needs the moon?
You are the stars! Who needs the stars?
O cling to me little baby in this broken dream
And let me protect you from this evil

Evil! Evil! Evil! Evil!

Kitchenette

I keep hanging around your kitchenette
And I'm gonna get a pot to cook you in
I stick my fingers in your biscuit jar
And crush all your gingerbread men
Cause I want you
Yeah, I want you to be my friend
Yeah, I want you
Yeah, I want to be your solitary man

Try not to wake the executioner
He's sleeping with a fireman's axe
He leaves his glass eye on the pillow, babe
And his dentures floating there in a glass
Makes it hard to relax!
Makes it hard to relax!
When I want you
I want you to be my friend

Ah it's getting hard to relax!
It's getting hard to get my act together!

What's this husband of yours ever given to you
Oprah Winfrey on a plasma screen
And a brood of jug-eared buck-toothed imbeciles
The ugliest kids I've ever seen
Oh baby I want you
I want you to be my girlfriend

Maybe we could send those kids to play down on the street
Hey, shouldn't you put shoes on their feet?
It's getting hard to relax
It's getting hard to relax

Gonna open up the window
Who's that coming up the back stairs?
Tippy-toe tippy-toe tippy-toe tippy-toe
Coming up the back stairs

I can see that you don't really dig him
And I can see that you want it to quit
But if you want to get your hand out of the cookie jar
You gonna have to let go of the biscuit
O babe I want you
I want you to be my girlfriend
Yeah, I want you
Yeah, I want to be your solitary man
I wanna be that man!

Palaces of Montezuma

Psychedelic invocations
Of Mata Hari at the station
I give to you
A Java princess of Hindu birth
A woman of flesh, a child of the earth
I give to you
The hanging gardens of Babylon
Miles Davis, the black unicorn
I give to you
The Palaces of Montezuma
And the gardens of Akbar's Tomb
I give to you
The Spider Goddess and the Needle Boy
And the slave-dwarves that they employ
I give to you
A custard-coloured super-dream
Of Ali McGraw and Steve McQueen
I give to you

C'mon baby, let's get out of the cold
And gimme gimme gimme your precious love
For me to hold

The Epic of Gilgamesh
A pretty little black A-line dress
I give to you
The spinal cord of JFK
Wrapped in Marilyn Monroe's negligee
I give to you
I want nothing in return
Just the softest little breathless word
I ask of you

A word contained in a grain of sand
That can barely walk, can't even stand
I ask for you

C'mon baby, let's get out of the cold
And gimme gimme gimme your precious love
For me to hold
C'mon baby, come out of the cold
And gimme gimme gimme your precious love
For me to hold

Bellringer Blues

I saw my old friend Gabriel
Down the perimeter ringing a bell
I said hello
Hey man is there something wrong?
Where has everybody gone?
I don't know
Well, I put my hand across my mouth
And I went out
Yeah, moving slow
What are you doing he said to me
I'm looking for my company
He said don't bother, no

Well, next thing you know when I took a look
Gabe was trying to sell me a book
But I got no dough
He said check it out, it's going cheap
Check it out, it's going cheap
I'll give it a go
Well, I read that book, every page
And then I put it away
Said I don't think so
It makes slaves of all of womankind
And corpses of the men
And I just don't know

And we care a little bit
And we get scared a little bit
Of those two cold dead eyes that stare a little bit
And we cry a little bit
And we get by a little bit
Let your tears all come falling down

Put me on a big white steed
Ride it up and down your street
Wrapped up in a crimson coat
Sail me in a great big boat
I'll sail around the waters for you
Kill your sons and daughters for you
Put me on a big white horse
Send me down to Banbury Cross

It's okay Joe it's time to go!
It's okay Joe it's time to go!
It's okay Joe it's time to go!
It's okay Joe it's time to go!

Push the Sky Away (2013)

We No Who U R
Wide Lovely Eyes
Water's Edge
Jubilee Street
Mermaids
We Real Cool
Finishing Jubilee Street
Higgs Boson Blues
Push the Sky Away
Needle Boy
Lightning Bolts

We No Who U R

The tree don't care what the little bird sings
We go down with the dew in the morning
The tree don't know what the little bird brings
We go down with the dew in the morning

And we breathe it in
There is no need to forgive
Breathe it in
There is no need to forgive

The trees will stand like pleading hands
We go down with the dew in the morning light
The trees all stand like pleading hands
We go down with the dew in the morning

And we breathe it in
There is no need to forgive
Breathe it in
There is no need to forgive

The trees will burn like blackened hands
We return with the light of the evening
The trees will burn like blackened hands
There's nowhere to rest, there's nowhere to land

And we know who you are
And we know where you live
And we know there's no need to forgive

And we know who you are
And we know where you live
And we know there's no need to forgive

And we know who you are
And we know where you live
And we know there's no need to forgive

And we know who you are
And we know where you live
And we know there's no need to forgive

Wide Lovely Eyes

You wave at the sky with wide lovely eyes
Waves and waves of love goodbye
Through the garden with your secret key
Down the tunnel that leads to the sea
Step onto the beach
Beneath the iron skies
You wave and wave with your wide lovely eyes
Crystal waves and waves of love
You wave and say goodbye

Your dress sighs with your wide lovely strides
All along the street and lately the stories abound
They've dismantled the funfair
And shut down the rides
And they've hung the mermaids from the street lights by their hair
With wide lovely eyes you wave at the sky
And me at the high window watching you ride
The waves of blue and the waves of love
You wave and say goodbye

The night expands I am expanding
I watch your hands like butterflies landing
All among the myths and the legends we create
And all the laughing stories we tell our friends
Close the windows, clear up the mess, it's getting late
It's dark and closer to the end
And through the tunnel and down to the sea
And on the pebble beach your laces you untie
And arrange your shoes side by side
You wave and wave with wide lovely eyes
Distant waves and waves of distant love
You wave and say goodbye

Water's Edge

They take apart their bodies like toys for the local boys
Because they're always there at the edge of the water
They come from the capital these city girls
Go way down where the stones meet the sea

And all you young girls, where do you hide?
Down by the water and the restless tide

And the local boys hide on the mound and watch
Reaching for the speech and the word to be heard
And the boys grow hard, hard to be heard
Hard to be heard as they reach for the speech
And search for the word on the water's edge

But you grow old and you grow cold
Yeah you grow old and you grow cold

And they would come in their hoards these city girls
With white strings flowing from their ears
As the local boys behind the mound
Think long and hard about the girls from the capital
Who dance at the water's edge shaking their asses

And all you young lovers where do you hide?
Down by the water and the restless tide

With a bible of tricks they do with their legs
The girls reach for the speech and the speech to be heard
To be hard the local boys teem down the mound
And seize the girls from the capital
Who shriek at the edge of the water
Shriek to speak and reach for the speech
Yeah reach for the speech and be heard

But you grow old and you grow cold
Yeah you grow old and you grow cold
You grow old

Their legs wide to the world like bibles open
To be speared and taking their bodies apart like toys
They dismantle themselves by the water's edge
And reach for the speech and the wide wide world
And, God knows, the local boys

It's the will of love
It's the thrill of love
Ah but the chill of love
Is comin' on

It's the will of love
It's the thrill of love
Ah but the chill of love
Is comin' on

It's the will of love
It's the thrill of love
Ah but the chill of love
Is comin' down, people

Jubilee Street

On Jubilee Street
There was a girl named Bee
She had a history
But she had no past
When they shut her down
The Russians moved in
I'm too scared, I'm too scared
To even walk on past
She used to say
All those good people
Down on Jubilee Street
They ought to practice what they preach
Yeah they ought to practice what they preach
Those good people
On Jubilee Street

And here I come up the hill
I'm pushing my wheel of love
I got love in my tummy
And a tiny little pain
And a ten ton catastrophe
On a sixty pound chain
And I'm pushing
My wheel of love up Jubilee Street
Oh look at me now

The problem was
She had a little black book
And my name was written on every page
Well a girl's got to make ends meet
Even down on Jubilee Street

I was out of place and time
And over the hill
And out of my mind
On Jubilee Street
I ought to practice what I preach

These days I go down town
In my tie and tails
I got a foetus on a leash
I am alone now
I am beyond recriminations
The curtains are shut
The furniture has gone
I am transforming
I am vibrating
I am glowing
I am flying
Look at me now
I am flying
Look at me now

Mermaids

She was a catch
We were a match
I was the match
That would fire up her snatch
But there was a catch
I was no match
I was fired from her crotch
Now I sit around and watch
The mermaids sun themselves
Out on the rocks
They are beyond our touch
I watch and watch
Them wave at me
They wave at me
They wave and slip
Back into the sea

All the ones who come
And all the ones who go
Down to the water

All the ones who come
And all the ones who go
Down to the sea

I believe in God
I believe in mermaids too
I believe in seventy-two virgins
On a chain why not why not
I believe in the rapture
For I've seen your face
On the floor of the ocean
At the bottom of the rain

I do driver alertness course
I do husband alertness course
I do mermaid alertness course
I watch them out on the rocks
They wave at me
They wave at me
They wave and slip
Back into the sea

All the ones who come
And all the ones who go
Down to the water

All the ones who come
And the ones who go
Down to the sea

We Real Cool

Who took your measurements
From your toes to the top of your head?
You know
Who bought you clothes and new shoes
And wrote you a book you never read?
Yeah, you know

Who was it?
Yeah, you know we real cool
On the far side of the morning
Who was it?
Yeah, you know we real cool
Ah I hope you're listening
Are you?

Who was it you called the good shepherd
Rounding up the kids for their meal?
Who chased your shadow running out behind?
Clinging to your high flying heels
Your high flying, high flying, high flying heels

Who was it?
Yeah, you know we real cool
On the far side of the morning
Who was it?
Yeah, you know we real cool
And I hope you're listening
Are you?

Who measured the distance from the planets
Right down to your big blue spinning world?
In heartbeats and tears and nervous laughter
Spilling down all over you, girl

Who was it?
Yeah, you know we real cool
And the world keeps on turning
Who was it?
Yeah, you know we real cool
And I hope you're listening
Are you?

Sirius is eight-point-six light years away
Arcturus is thirty-seven
The past is the past
And it's here to stay
Wikipedia is heaven
When you don't want to remember no more
On the far side of the morning
Who was it?

Yeah, you know we real cool
I hope you hear me
And you'll call

Finishing Jubilee Street

I just finished writing Jubilee Street
I lay down on my bed and fell into a deep sleep
And when I awoke I believed
I had taken a bride called Mary Stanford
And I flew into a frenzy searching high and low
Because in my dream the girl was very young

I said 'hey little girl, where do you hide?'
You draw lightning from the sky

All of this in her dark hair
All of this in her dark hair oh Lord

See that girl comin' on down
See that girl comin' on down

Last night your shadow scampered up the wall it fly
And leaped like a black spider between your legs
And cried
My children! My children!
They are lost to us

All of this in her dark hair
All of this in her dark hair oh Lord

See that girl comin' on down
See that girl comin' on down

Higgs Boson Blues

Can't remember anything at all
Flame trees lined the streets
Can't remember anything at all
But I'm driving my car down to Geneva

I've been sitting in my basement patio
It was hot
Up above the girls walk past
Their roses all in bloom

Have you ever heard about the Higgs Boson Blues?
I'm going down to Geneva baby
Gonna teach it to you

Who cares?
Who cares what the future brings?

Black road long and I drove and drove
Came upon a crossroad
The night was hot and black
I see Robert Johnson
With a ten dollar guitar
Strapped to his back
Looking for a tune
Ah, well here comes Lucifer with his canon law
And a hundred black babies running from his genocidal jaw
He got the real killer groove
Robert Johnson and the devil, man
Don't know who's gonna rip off who

Driving my car
Flame trees on fire
Sitting and singing
The Higgs Boson Blues

I'm tired, I'm looking for a spot to drop
All the clocks have stopped in Memphis
And the Lorraine Motel is hot
It's hot, that's why they call it the hot spot
I take a room with a view
Hear a man preaching in a language that's completely new
Making the hot cots in the flop house bleed
While the cleaning ladies sob into their mops
And the bellhop hops and bops
As a shot rings out to a spiritual groove
Everybody bleeding
To the Higgs Boson Blues

And if I die tonight
Bury me in my favourite yellow patent leather shoes
And with a mummified cat
And a cone-like hat
That the Caliphate forced on the Jews

Can you feel my heart beat?
Can you feel my heart beat?

Hannah Montana does the African Savannah
As the simulated rainy season begins
She curses the queue at the zoo loos
And moves on to Amazonia
Cries with the dolphins

The Mai-Mai eat the pigmy, the pigmy eat the monkey
The monkey has a gift that he is sending back to you
Look! Here come the missionary
With his smallpox and flu
Saving them savages with his Higgs Boson Blues

I'm driving my car down to Geneva
I'm driving my car down to Geneva

Oh let the damn day break
Rainy days always make me sad
Miley Cyrus floats in a swimming pool in Taluca Lake
And you're the best girl I ever had

Can't remember anything at all

Push the Sky Away

I was riding, I was riding
The sun was rising up from the fields

I got a feeling I just can't shake
I got a feeling that just won't go away

You've gotta just keep on pushing
And keep on pushing
Push the sky away

And if your friends think that you should do it different
And if they think that you should do it the same

You've gotta just keep on pushing
And keep on pushing
Push the sky away

And if you feel you got everything you came for
If you got everything and you don't want no more
You've gotta just keep on pushing
And keep on pushing
Push the sky away

And some people say it's just rock and roll
Oh but it gets you right down to your soul
You've gotta just keep on pushing
And keep on pushing
Push the sky away

You've gotta just keep on pushing
And keep on pushing
Push the sky away

Needle Boy

At the turn of the century I did many things to protect myself
I did many things to protect myself
I made myself a needle boy
And I hid him in the closet
And I made myself a money man
And I hid him underneath a mattress
And I made myself a spider child
And I put him in a matchbox
And I forged myself a golden statuette
And I wrapped him up in a *Hello* magazine
And I hid him in a wall safe
And finally I made myself a spade girl
And I put her in a garden shed
All to protect myself you see
From the demon that was comin' from the east
Or from the west
And then I sat on the rooftop and I waited

And when at last the demon came
From the east or from the west
And awoke me from my sleep
And awake me to a particular point of view
And the needle boy stuck him in the eye
And the money man chocked him with coins
The spider child bit him on the ankle
And the statuette crashed down upon his head
And the spade girl buried him underneath the house
And I danced on the rooftops
And I danced on the rooftops
And I danced to the western world
And I danced to the western world

Lightning Bolts

Two lightning bolts were delivered to my room
They were gifts from Zeus
I rock the bolts in a bassinet of pine
People ask me how I am
I say I'm alright, I'm fine

I push the lightning bolts in a pram
Till the sun goes down and it gets dark
And the girls from Jubilee Street hang out their windows
And they wave and ask me how I am tonight
I say I'm good, I'm alright

In Athens all the youths are crying from the gas
I'm by the hotel pool, working on a tan
People come up and ask me who I am
I say if you don't know, don't ask
Zeus laughs, but it's the gas
And he asks me how I am
I say Zeus, don't ask

My lightning bolts are jolts of joy
They are joy boys from Zeus
I feed them porridge in their booster seats of knowledge
And in the cradle of democracy
The pigeons are wearing gas masks

My lightning bolts play in the elevators
They slide down the hotel banister
And Zeus throws a gas canister
And it spins around the pool
As pigeons wearing respirators steal the lightning bolts

Zeus wants them back
Oh my bolts of joy
Oh my darling little boys
They are lost to us

Young people, they are never coming back
At night I watch them sleep
And cry years of tears
But it's not the gas
People ask me how we are
We are, I say, mostly lost

Index of Titles

Index of First Lines

He just wanted a decent book to read …

Not too much to ask, is it? It was in 1935 when Allen Lane, Managing Director of Bodley Head Publishers, stood on a platform at Exeter railway station looking for something good to read on his journey back to London. His choice was limited to popular magazines and poor-quality paperbacks – the same choice faced every day by the vast majority of readers, few of whom could afford hardbacks. Lane's disappointment and subsequent anger at the range of books generally available led him to found a company – and change the world.

'We believed in the existence in this country of a vast reading public for intelligent books at a low price, and staked everything on it'
Sir Allen Lane, 1902–1970, founder of Penguin Books

The quality paperback had arrived – and not just in bookshops. Lane was adamant that his Penguins should appear in chain stores and tobacconists, and should cost no more than a packet of cigarettes.

Reading habits (and cigarette prices) have changed since 1935, but Penguin still believes in publishing the best books for everybody to enjoy. We still believe that good design costs no more than bad design, and we still believe that quality books published passionately and responsibly make the world a better place.

So wherever you see the little bird – whether it's on a piece of prize-winning literary fiction or a celebrity autobiography, political tour de force or historical masterpiece, a serial-killer thriller, reference book, world classic or a piece of pure escapism – you can bet that it represents the very best that the genre has to offer.

Whatever you like to read – trust Penguin.

read more
www.penguin.co.uk